MW01408017

CORAZÓN CONTENTO

Sonoran Recipes and Stories from the Heart

CORAZÓN CONTENTO
Sonoran Recipes and Stories from the Heart

Madeline Gallego Thorpe

Mary Tate Engels

Introduction by Patricia Preciado Martin

Texas Tech University Press

© Copyright 1999 Texas Tech University Press

All rights reserved. No portion of this book may be reproduced in any form or by any means, including electronic storage and retrieval systems, except by explicit, prior written permission of the publisher except for brief passages excerpted for review and critical purposes.

This book was set in Lapidary 333 and Davidian. The paper used in this book meets the minimum requirements of ANSI/NISO Z39.48-1992 (R1997). ∞

Design by Melissa Bartz

Printed in the United States of America

Library of Congress Cataloging-in-Publication Data
Engels, Mary Tate.
    Corazón contento : Sonoran recipes and stories from the heart / Mary Tate Engels and Madeline Gallego Thorpe.
      p. cm.
    ISBN 0-89672-417-4 (cloth : alk. paper)
    1. Cookery. American–Southwestern style. 2. Cookery—Arizona—Tucson. I. Thorpe. Madeline Gallego. II. Title.
TX715.2.S69E53   1999
641.59791—dc21   99-10804
                                                   CIP

99 00 01 02 03 04 05 06 07 / 9 8 7 6 5 4 3 2

Texas Tech University Press
Box 41037
Lubbock, Texas 79409-1037 USA
800-832-4042
ttup@ttu.edu
Http://www.ttup.ttu.edu

CONTENTS

Introduction by Patricia Preciado Martin	vii
Acknowledgments	xi
De Mi Corazón—From My Heart	1
Love and the Art of Cooking	3
SPICY SPRING	5
SIMMERING SUMMER	33
FLAVORS OF FALL	69
WINTER COMFORTS	107
Full Circle	140
Index	143

INTRODUCTION

According to conventional wisdom, our ability to smell is of the five senses not only the most enduring, but the most evocative. Who has not experienced, upon encountering the familiar aroma of a favorite food, the sensation of being transported back to the idyllic and comforting time of childhood? This is eloquently evidenced in the reminiscences of Sra. Esperanza Montoya Padilla, whom I interviewed for my book *Songs My Mother Sang to Me: An Oral History of Mexican American Women*. Doña Esperanza was born in the small mining town of Southeastern Arizona in 1915. The memory of her mother's cooking has influenced and sustained her throughout all her life:

> As long as I can remember, my mother always had a boarding house. The boarding house was always part of our home. There were trees all around—fruit trees mostly. My mother made jam. And they had animals, of course . . . goats, and a cow for fresh milk and pigs and chickens and even turkeys. . . . When my father slaughtered a pig, my mother would make *carne adobada*. She made a sauce with red chile, garlic, onions, oregano and other spices and then dipped the meat in the sauce and let it drain and dry. I remember, also, that when an animal was slaughtered, they collected the blood and they would take it to Mother in the kitchen. She put garlic and onion in it and then she cooked it and stirred it until it was thickened and curdled. It looked like chopped liver. They made *chicharrones,* also. They cut up the pork skins outside and then cooked them in a kettle on an open fire. Everyone pitched in. There was a lot of action! I tell my kids that I love all those foods because I was raised with them.
>
> My mother was a very good cook and she could make almost anything—American as well as Mexican style food. She made a lot of *guisados* and *caldos,* and of course, tortillas. She had to make pies and cakes and cupcakes for the miners' lunches. She made the best *empanadas de calabaza!* In fact, I still make them myself, but I wonder if I'm doing it the right way. . . .

Mother would get up very early and put on the coffee and make breakfast and pack lunches for the men. She made fried eggs and potato.... She made her own chorizo. She also made pancakes and baking powder biscuits in the mornings. And then, of course, she had to get an early start on the evening meal.

In the evenings, after dinner, that's when she baked bread and rolls. I guess that's when she had the time. When it was Mother's rest time, she would sit down in her chair. I don't know what she was thinking. I was little, running around, jumping around—and she would say to me, *"Abre el horno para ver como está el pan."* "Go open the oven door and see how the bread is doing." And I would go and look and then go tell her that it looked this way or that.... My kids always say that I make the best bread, But I still think my mother's was better. Maybe it's because when you are a child everything your mother makes tastes so good....

I have two kitchens and *remadas* all over the place. I do my heavy cooking—bread and pies and menudo—on the porch. My kids tell me that I'm always thinking about food. I guess that I inherited that from my mother. When we lived in Mascot there were always people coming and going to the mine and they would go by our house. Mother would always take out the empanadas or the cookies and coffee. So (now) everybody that comes to our house—I fix them something to eat. I don't know what it is with me—I always have to be making food and goodies for my family.[1]

The memory is the rock upon which her world and her *alma* is built. And as so poignantly sensed in her story—and indeed in the stories of all of us who hearken back to the scenes in our mother's kitchens, the *antojo*—the craving for the food is indistinguishable from the yearning we have for our Madre's *presencia* and the days of yore.

As a case in point, I would like to add that some of my fondest childhood memories revolve around my mother Aurelia, her *cocina,* and the wonderful aromas that greeted me every day as I returned from school. Those delicious fragrances wafting out of the front door of our humble adobe house—as I parked my bicycle against the porch post hot and tired and sometimes dismayed after a not-so-great day at school—said to me, "I'm glad you're home." The first thing that I would do as I entered the kitchen would be to peek into the pan or pot or oven to check on what was cooking. And if Mother was not looking, I'd snitch a spoonful of this or that. I'd sit at the kitchen table that was the center of our family life, eat hot buttered tortillas off the grill as fast as she could make them, and recount the day's events as she went about her dinner chores.[2] She'd listen thoughtfully to my woes and triumphs, adding philosophy, advice, proverbs and observations about life to the flavor of my day, just as deftly as she added seasonings to the soups and stews and sauces. She understood instinctively—as did many of our *madres* and *abuelas*—that food was not just sustenance for the body, but just as importantly—nourishment for the soul.

The women of our mothers' and grandmothers' generations prided themselves on their domestic skills and their cooking abilities. Most of their waking hours, it would seem in retrospect, were dedicated to their craft. And although Mexican food is now considered to be one of the five great "cuisines" in the world, they wouldn't have recognized the word in any language. The tools of their art—for art it was—were simple and basic: wooden spoons; a good knife; a *molcajete;* a *comal;* a few battered saucepans; cast iron frying pans; a vintage stove; and as in the case of Doña Esperanza's mother, and my own grandmothers, a woodburning stove and an icebox instead of a refrigerator. They had no bread machines, no gourmet cooking sets with teflon coating, no food processors, no microwaves, no "fast food," no instant anything.

Upon reflection, then, our *madres* and *abuelitas* intuited what many of us in our and the younger generation are just beginning to understand: that bread is only the staff of life when it is made with unconditional love and leavened with the finite gift of time gladly given.

Patricia Preciado Martin

[1]*Songs My Mother Sang to Me: An Oral History of Mexican American Women,* Patricia Preciado Martin (Tucson: University of Arizona Press, 1992); 102-106, 116-117.
[2]From *Tucson Mexican Restaurants: Repasts, Recipes and Remembrances,* Suzanne Myal (Tucson: Fiesta Publishing, 1997); 69. By permission of the author.

ACKNOWLEDGMENTS

We would like to thank a group of friends and family who met in the fall of 1996 to discuss the possibility of a book containing Madeline's wonderful recipes. Bea Anne Berg, Sally Freund, Toni Saccani, Jean Dalton, Carol McLemore, and Stephanie Engels have been our constant supporters in the creation of this book.

Thanks also to Madeline's family, who helped by supplying information and photos. A special thanks to Kathy Lacarona, Madeline's aunt, who was there for us at every turn, who helped Madeline remember these marvelous stories, and who contributed a few of her own.

And, of course, we want to thank our close friends with whom we have played, partied, and traveled extensively, and with whom we have made our tamales each December for so many years: Sally and Jerry Freund, Toni and Tino Saccani, Martha and David Preston, and our husbands, Darrell Thorpe and Roger Engels. They have all helped to carry on these traditions. *Gracias a todos!* You would make Magdalena and Gabriel proud. And so would this book.

Corazón Contento, Sonoran Recipes and Stories from the Heart, is dedicated to the memory of my grandparents, Gabriel and Magdalena Contreras. I want to thank them for welcoming me into their home after having raised nine children of their own. What they may have lacked in material things, they made up in kindness, love, pride, and respect for tradition. It is from them that I learned the recipes, remedies, and sayings that are the basis for this book.

MGT

Es nuestra esperanza que nuestros hijos, y sus hijos,
continúen manteniendo nuestras tradiciones con orgullo.
We hope that our children and their children will continue observing our traditions with pride.

Scattered throughout the recipes are:

◆ *Dichos* — sayings or little diamonds of wisdom scattered among the recipes.
❀ *Remedios* — medicinal remedies, usually made from plants, mingling with the recipes.
❤ *Recuerdos* — stories from the heart about life in the Old Pueblo, or Tucson, to bring the recipes home.

Panza Llena, Corazón Contento
Full Stomach, Contented Heart

De Mi Corazón
From My Heart

♥ I grew up with my grandparents, Magdalena and Gabriel Contreras, in Tucson, Arizona. When I was seven months old, my mother and father went to California to find work, because at that time jobs were not abundant in Tucson. Once established, they planned to return for me, but childcare was a problem, since they both worked. Besides, by then, my grandparents insisted that I stay with them. I'm sure it was a difficult decision for Mom and Dad, but it allowed me to experience the rich Mexican-American culture in Tucson during the late 1940s and '50s.

My grandparents' love and influence on my life were great. From my grandfather, I learned patience, and compassion, and the ability to have a listening ear. He showed me how to savor life, to "enjoy every spoonful." My grandmother, on the other hand, dished out spice and zest. She was a strong woman and would tell me, "You can do anything in this world, because we're all capable." She showed me how to be thrifty and how to cook, and gave me the self-esteem necessary to walk boldly on new ground. They both knew how to enjoy life and passed that treasure on to me also.

When the family gathered, we always had a table filled with festive food. After dinner, we would sing, dance, and play instruments. Our family had lots of fun. Uncle Eddie played the piano and told corny jokes. He did a soft-shoe routine in the middle of the living room and tried to teach us, but we kids never could get the steps right. Uncle Gilbert played the guitar and sang, while Uncle John played the saxophone. My mom, Margaret, had a beautiful voice and dreamed of being a singer with a big band. She would often sing *Por un Amor* to my dad. Grandfather, *Abuelito,* loved to dance, and sometimes would dance by himself at these celebrations. Grandmother, *Abuelita,* could sing and accompany herself on the piano or guitar. As my grandparents got older, their children would entertain them with music, and they loved it.

Over the years, I have continued the traditions of my Arizona-Sonora roots by preparing the foods of my heritage for my family and friends. Since I often cook from memory, friends and family have begged me to write down the recipes. But, as I began to record the *recetas,* memories of my childhood days came flooding back: memories of the people, the events, the places, and the wonderful times. It was impossible to separate the food from the *recuerdos,* those stories from my heart. Many of the ingredients in the recipes reminded me of the *remedios,* the remedies based on plants and herbs that my Abuelita used for healing her family and friends. To this day, I can also still hear her *dichos,* or sayings, diamonds of advice for life delivered with both wisdom and wit. One of her favorites was *Panza llena, corazón contento,* "Full stomach, contented heart," and, certainly, she always made sure we had plenty to eat. I can see Abuelito showing his love in his own special way, telling us ghost stories, and sharing his famous *teswin* with his neighbors. So here, in this book, are the foods, the attitudes, the spice, the love, and the compassion of my youth for you all to enjoy.

Love and the Art of Cooking

Cooking is a sensuous art and should not be restricted by either the recipe or by your own fear to try something. For me, cooking is a thoroughly pleasurable experience. There is natural pleasure in the eating of good food. And there is the sociable pleasure in sharing what you have prepared, and in having people enjoy both the time together and the food. But the real art is in the preparation. While you're cooking, taste what you're making, and be sure to add more spices if needed. Spices open the senses, so don't spare them. If you like more flavor than the recipe calls for, go for the gusto.

In most of my recipes, the directions read, "salt to taste." That's because some people can't eat any salt, while others have a stronger taste for it. Remember, it's up to you. If you feel like adding a handful of any ingredient, go for it!

At times I thought some of my grandmother's dishes were too salty. If I said something about it, Abuelita would say, "Too salty? I must have been especially happy today." So, since I'm happy most of the time, I tend to be heavy-handed with the salt. But you should cook the way you feel. Don't be afraid to experiment. And enjoy the love and art of cooking, and the pleasure of eating!

Mi Vida

Qué linda es mi vida.
Qué linda fue mi juventud.
De mis abuelitos,
   los dichos que son mis diamantitos,
   las memorias que llenan mi corazón,
   las recetas y los remedios,
   las viejas amistades del barrio de mi juventud.
Gracias a mis abuelitos por mi dulce vida.

My Life

How beautiful is my life.
How beautiful was my youth.
From my grandparents
   the sayings that are my little diamonds,
   the memories that fill my heart,
   the recipes and the remedies,
   the old friends from the neighborhood of my youth.
Thank you, my grandparents, for my sweet life.

SPICY SPRING

Spring vacillates between the surprise of winter's coolness and the promise of summer's warmth. Occasionally a winter storm tops the mountains surrounding Tucson with a cap of snow, threatening us with a late frost. But the threat is weak, and soon all of nature welcomes the return of a beautiful desert spring. The birds awaken their world at dawn, busy in their nesting pursuits. Pairs of Gambel's quails, topknot feathers bobbling, wander through the cactus, and soon lead a procession of identical chicks.

Nature's conservative browns and greens revive with the colorful blooms of cacti and other desert plants—bright yellow or red prickly pear, magenta hedgehog, and red-orange ocotillo. The giant saguaro wears a crown of large white flowers as if to proclaim itself king of plants. Both the indigenous people of the area and the early Hispanic settlers found many uses for these and other native plants.

Citrus trees release the sweet, unmistakable fragrance of orange blossoms that, along with herbs, are often used for *remedios*. Desert wild flowers join the bright bougainvillea and other domesticated flowering plants in prolific displays of color.

The sunrise beckons each day with pinks and violets streaking across the morning skies. People, through religious ceremony, song, dance, and special food, celebrate the eternal promise of rebirth. The Lenten season culminates with Easter, and a string of celebrations in the city parks almost every weekend include music, dance, art, and food. The Pascua Yaqui Indians' Easter celebrations, numerous arts and crafts fairs, *Cinco de Mayo* events, and the 4th Avenue Street Fair are just a few of the regional festivities. Mexican American families throughout the Southwest traditionally serve many of these spring dishes created from the bounty of the land and associated with the religious observances surrounding Easter.

Capirotada
Bread Pudding

16 oz. *piloncillo* or *panocha** (or substitute 2 cups regular brown sugar)
¼ cup green onion, chopped
¼ cup cilantro, chopped
2 cinnamon sticks
6 cloves
4 or 5 cups water
1 lb. loaf French or Italian bread
1 large banana, sliced thin
1 large apple, peeled, cored, and sliced thin
1 cup raisins
1 cup peanuts
8 oz. sharp cheddar cheese, grated
½ cup butter

In a medium saucepan, make a syrup using water, piloncillo, cinnamon sticks, cloves, green onions and cilantro. Cook over medium heat until the piloncillo has dissolved. While your syrup is simmering on low, go ahead and prepare the rest of the ingredients. The syrup will be ready in about 10 minutes, or when sugar and spices have mingled.

Butter the bread and brown on both sides under the broiler. In a glass baking dish, layer the toasted bread (broken into pieces), apple, banana, raisins, peanuts and cheese. Alternate all ingredients, ending with a cheese layer. Strain out the spices from the syrup, then pour syrup over the layers in the baking dish. Bake for 30 minutes at 325°.

**Piloncillo or panocha* is unrefined brown sugar that is pressed into small loaves or cones. Sizes and weights may vary.

Spicy Spring

❤ This is a traditional Lenten dish. The marriage of the different flavors gives it a taste that is exciting and sensuous. When the air was cool and crisp outside, Abuelita would gather all her ingredients and start making the capirotada. The wonderful aromas from the kitchen enticed us, and we could hardly wait for it to finish cooking.

❀ *Clavos* (cloves)

Add 2 or 3 cloves to any tea to help reduce abdominal cramps. A clove dipped in oil and placed in the cavity where a tooth has been pulled will reduce the pain of the extraction.

Abuelito and Abuelita on their wedding day, about 1912.
He was around 19 years old; she was a year younger.

Carne Asada
Grilled Steak

Abuelita would rub her steaks with garlic, salt, and olive oil. Then, Abuelito would grill them outside over a wood fire. Wonderful with a watercress salad or the salad of your choice.

❤ Often we went to midnight Mass the night before Easter. On Easter Sunday, we got up very early and made the trip from Tucson to Patagonia, a little town about sixty miles southeast of the city, for an all-day family picnic. Sometimes someone would go early and get us a good shady spot close to the water on Patagonia Lake. When we arrived, we'd start an open fire and make egg burritos with green chiles or chorizo, and *café con leche*. This was a special celebration that marked the end of the personal sacrifices of Lent—for traditionally, each of us would have given up something for the duration of the Lenten season—and we ate continuously all day: chile beans, macaroni and potato salads, watermelon, and desserts. Later we'd prepare carne asada, and eat it with tortillas and *pan de huevo*.

Several men brought guitars, and we sang all the good old *rancheras* (the traditional "country" songs of Mexico) and other songs, such as *Paloma Blanca* and *La Múcura* until dark. My mom and her two sisters, my *tías*, entertained everyone with their beautiful harmony on *Baraja Marcada, Por un Amor,* and Abuelita's favorite, *La Paloma*. We kids would catch guppies in the lake and bring them home, hoping the poor things would live. But they never did.

Aunt Kathy, in her early 20s, playing her guitar on a beautiful spring day about 1958.

Carne Seca con Huevos

Dried Meat and Eggs

1½ cups *carne seca* (See p. 41)
2 eggs
½ onion, minced
2 jalapeños, roasted, peeled, seeded and chopped
   (roasting and peeling optional)
1 tomato, chopped
3 Tbsp. cilantro, chopped
2 Tbsp. olive oil
salt to taste

Put olive oil in a frying pan, warm it, and add the carne seca. Turn heat to medium and add onion, jalapeños, tomato and cilantro. When this mixture is sizzling, add your two eggs and scramble. I usually figure on ¼ to ½ cup carne seca per person. But since this is a generous and tasty meat, you can simply add more eggs to feed more people. Serve with corn or flour tortillas. This dish is well-complemented by slices of fresh ripe mangoes.

You can also use this mixture to roll in soft corn or flour tortillas for breakfast or lunch burritos. Also, you can omit the eggs and just make a carne seca burrito or taco.

❤ When I was a baby, everyone doted on me because I was the only little one in my grandparents' house. They nicknamed me *Neka* or *Nekita,* short for *Muñeca,* which means "doll." My family still calls me *Neka*.

♥ *Cuando cobraba su salario, mi tío Gabe cambiaba su cheque y me rociaba con dinero, cuando yo estaba acostadita en mi camita. Me decía, "Nekita, esto es para desearte mucho dinero y buena suerte en tu futuro, y que nunca te haga falta nada en tu vida." Luego me cogía en sus brazos, y me cubría de besitos. Es verdad que yo tuve mucho amor en nuestra familia tan grande.*

Uncle Gabe would cash his pay check and shower me with dollars as I lay in my crib. He would say: *"Nekita,* this is to wish you lots of money and good luck in your future; may you never lack for anything in your life." Then he would pick me up and cover me with kisses. Obviously, I had lots of love in this big family.

♦ *Dime con quien andas, y te diré quien eres.*
Tell me who you walk with, and I'll tell you who you are.

Uncle Gabe, in his military uniform during World War II.

Spicy Spring

Abuelita, probably 66, stands in her garden about 1960; she especially loved her flowers.

Abuelito and Abuelita on his 70th birthday in 1964. He loved to have his photo taken.

Pollo en Chile Colorado
Chicken in Red Chile

8 chicken breasts
2 cloves garlic
3 Tbsp. flour
2 bay leaves
sprinkle of vinegar
3 cups red chile sauce (canned, frozen, or made from your own *ristra*. See p. 56)
2 tsp. salt, or to taste

In a 2-qt. pot, put chicken breasts and garlic in 2 cups of water and cook over medium heat for 20 to 30 minutes. Reserve broth. Remove skin, debone chicken, cut meat into cubes, and let cool. Put chicken into a bag with a mixture of the flour and salt, and toss to coat. Warm the red chile sauce, add chicken and the bay leaves, and enough chicken broth to give you the consistency you want. Cook on low for about another 30 minutes.

❤ This is the favorite dish of both my husband Darrell and son Eric. I serve it with large flour tortillas, Spanish rice (see p. 25) and refried beans (see p. 94).

◆ *De joven ángel, de viejo diablo.*
Young saint, old devil.

Ejote en Chile Colorado

Green Beans with Red Chile

2 lbs. cooked green beans (fresh, frozen, or canned)
2 cups homemade chile sauce or 1 16-oz. can chile sauce
   (Las Palmas brand is my favorite)
2 egg whites
salt to taste

Warm green beans in their own liquid, then drain off liquid and add the chile sauce. Bring all to a boil, and add slightly beaten egg whites to thicken mixture. Stir while adding, and continue to cook until chile is the consistency you want. Add grated cheese of your choice, if desired. Serve as a side dish, as a main dish over rice, or rolled into a burrito.

❤ Abuelita often served this dish during Lent, which was a very serious religious time of the year for us, and remains so for many Catholic people in the Arizona/Sonora border area. We always give up something, usually food or drink, for the duration of the season, and try to improve ourselves during that time. When Easter finally comes, it is a time of celebration, both religious and personal. It represents a release from those self-imposed restrictions. Now you can eat all the things you gave up for Lent, and the day is spent in celebration.

Jericalla a la Madeline
Madeline's Meringue Custard

4 egg yolks
1 Tbsp. corn starch
½ cup sugar
¼ tsp. salt
2 cups milk
2 sticks cinnamon

In double boiler, mix egg yolks, cornstarch, ½ cup sugar, and salt, and cook over medium heat until thickened. In a different pan, scald the milk with the two cinnamon sticks for flavor, that is, warm it to just before the boiling point, but do not let it boil. Remove the cinnamon sticks, and add the scalded milk slowly to the egg mixture, stirring constantly. Pour into custard cups and top with meringue. (See recipe below.) Bake at 400° for a few minutes until meringue is golden brown. Watch it carefully, because it won't take long. Serve warm or cold, as you like. I prefer mine chilled.

Meringue

4 egg whites
1 Tbsp. sugar
¼ tsp. cinnamon

Whip egg whites by hand or with an electric mixer until they start to stiffen. Slowly add sugar and cinnamon and whip into peaks.

Jericalla de Abuelita
Abuelita's Jericalla

4 cups milk
1 cup sugar
1 cinnamon stick
6 eggs, beaten

 Mix the sugar and cinnamon stick into the milk and scald the milk (see previous recipe). Discard cinnamon stick and cool mixture a bit. Whisk beaten eggs into milk, stirring constantly to mix eggs thoroughly with the milk mixture. Pour mixture into a square 2-qt. glass baking dish, and place in a *baño de María* (bain-marie).* Bake at 350° for 40 to 45 minutes. Chill and serve.

*Baño de María is a method of slowing down the cooking of custard-like dishes, so they don't burn. The dish with the custard is placed in a larger flat pan filled with about an inch or two of hot water. This water should not be allowed to boil, so that your custard can cook slowly until firm. You may need to add water to the baño de María before the custard is finished cooking.

Nopales or *nopalitos* are the pads or leaves of the Burbank cactus, a variety of the prickly pear cactus. In the Southwest, they are available canned or they are sold in the produce or gourmet section of grocery stores.

♥ If you pick your own nopalitos, choose the new spring growth, which is the most tender and the best for cooking. (The same is true for picking the fruit from the prickly pear.) Scrape the stickers off the pads with a sharp knife, and wash the pads. Place them in salted, boiling water for about 20 minutes. Abuelita sliced an onion to boil with her nopalitos, because (like with okra) that helps hold the juices in the pads. After boiling, drain, and set the nopalitos aside for use. Preparation of nopalitos is the same for all the recipes included here. They must be dethorned, cleaned, and parboiled before using.

Nopalitos con Huevos

Nopalitos and Eggs

3 Tbsp. corn or olive oil
½ onion, chopped
1 cup cleaned and cooked nopalitos
4 eggs, beaten
corn or flour tortillas
salt to taste
salsa, homemade or bought, for flavor

Sauté chopped onion in oil over medium heat until onion is translucent. Cut nopalitos into thin strips, and sauté with onions a few minutes until tender. Add scrambled eggs and cook until firm. Serve scrambled egg mixture rolled in a tortilla or with the tortilla on the side. Add salsa if desired.

This is a basic nopalito recipe. Some people add fresh tomatoes, shrimp, fresh jalapeños, and cilantro. Try it the simple way first, and then let go and be creative.

Spicy Spring

◆ *Amigo beneficiado, enemigo declarado.*
Lend money to a friend and lose a friend.

The young pads of the Burbank cactus are used for nopalitos.

Nopalitos con Puerco
Nopalitos with Pork

8 nopalito pads, cleaned, parboiled, and cut into 1-inch strips
2 lbs. pork shoulder roast, cubed
3 Tbsp. vegetable oil
2 cloves garlic, minced
½ onion, finely chopped
3 cups red chile sauce (See p. 56)
2 Tbsp. flour

In a large skillet, brown cubed pork in a few tablespoons of oil. Add garlic and onion and sauté a couple of minutes; then add red chile sauce and simmer for about 40 minutes. Add nopalitos for the last 20 minutes of cooking along with your flour to make a thin chile gravy. (I keep flour in a shaker, like the ones for powdered sugar, and I just shake the flour into the liquid, stirring constantly. You can also dissolve the flour in a little liquid, and add that to the gravy.) Salt to taste and serve over steamed rice with corn tortillas and a tossed salad.

Ensalada de Nopalitos
Nopalito Salad

4 nopalito pads, cleaned, parboiled, and cut into 1-inch strips
½ lb. salad shrimp, cleaned, cooked, and peeled
½ medium red onion, sliced into thin rings
1 large tomato, cut into cubes
¼ cup cilantro, chopped
1 Tbsp. olive oil

In a large salad bowl, mix nopalitos, shrimp, tomato, and onion. Add olive oil, salt and pepper to taste. Cool before serving. Serves 4.

Pan de Huevo o Pan Dulce
Sweet Bread

1 tsp. yeast
3 Tbsp. melted butter or margarine
¼ cups water
2 eggs, slightly beaten
3½ cups flour
¼ cup sugar
pinch salt
cinnamon-flavored topping (see below)

Dissolve yeast in ¼ cup lukewarm water. Sift flour with sugar and salt into a different bowl. Add the yeast mixture, eggs, and butter and knead by hand. Place in a greased bowl, cover with a dry cotton cloth, and let rise in a warm place about 1 ½ hours or until it has doubled in bulk.

Place on a floured board and knead until smooth. Pinch off 2-inch balls of dough and place on a greased cookie sheet several inches apart. Flatten each ball down with your palm. Gently spread cinnamon topping over each bun, and let the buns rise until they double in bulk. Bake in preheated oven at 400° for 10 minutes or until lightly browned.

Cinnamon Topping

Blend together: 1 cup sugar, 1 cup sifted flour, 1 tsp. cinnamon, and a pinch of salt. Add ½ cup softened butter and 1 egg that has been slightly beaten.

◆ *Donde va Vicente, va la gente.*
Monkey see, monkey do.

❤ Abuelito taught us not to lie, cheat, or steal, and to help our neighbor, because he believed that whatever you do always comes back. He would say: "Do it because it warms your heart and makes you feel good."

He practiced what he preached. Once he was concerned about a friend whose wife had just left him. Abuelito feared the man was suicidal and wanted to do something to help, so he devised a remedy to keep the man busy. He gave his friend a small bag with seven seeds in it, and told him to take a seed out every day and pray for his wife to return. Then, he was to toss the seed into the air. Next, he instructed his friend to dig a hole in the front yard and place a pair of his wife's shoes in the hole, toes facing the house, as close to the door as he could. The friend thanked Abuelito for the remedy and seemed eager to try it. A few weeks later, he came to visit Abuelito, full of gratitude that his wife had returned.

Abuelito told me later that he had just made up the remedy to give his friend something active to do because he seemed so despondent. But, just in case, Abuelito said that he prayed every day for her return, too.

◆ *Donde hay amor, hay dolor.*
Where there is love, there is pain.

Pastel de Chocolate
Chocolate Cake

½ cup butter, softened
2 cups sugar
2 large eggs
4 oz. unsweetened chocolate, melted
1¾ cups all-purpose flour
1 tsp. baking powder
1 tsp. baking soda
¾ tsp. salt
1½ cups buttermilk
1 tsp. vanilla
1 tsp. cinnamon

Cream butter with an electric mixer and add sugar slowly. Add eggs one at a time and continue to mix. Add melted chocolate while it's still warm, and mix well.

Combine flour, baking powder, and baking soda, salt, and cinnamon. Alternate adding dry ingredients and buttermilk to the creamed butter mixture. Stir in vanilla. Pour batter into 9 × 13 in. pan. Bake at 350° for 30 to 35 minutes.

Fudge Frosting

6 oz. unsweetened chocolate, melted
¾ cup butter
5 cups powdered sugar
½ cup half-and-half
1 tsp. vanilla

In a small saucepan, melt chocolate and butter over low heat. In a mixing bowl, blend powdered sugar, half-and-half, and vanilla with the electric mixer at medium speed. Slowly add melted chocolate to milk mixture and beat until fluffy. Frost your cake.

Pollo Rojo en Hojas de Elote

Red Chile Chicken in Corn Husks

12 chicken legs (thighs and drumsticks)
6 cups red chile marinade (see below)
12 ears of corn for serving with meal
(Reserve 12 large corn husks for serving)

Clean corn of husks and silk. Save and rinse the husks; cook clean ears of corn later for meal. Prick chicken legs all over with a fork, and marinate with 2 cups of chile, about 2 hours on each side.

Line a large pot, such as the ones used for steaming tamales, with clean cornhusks on sides and bottom. Pour in 2 cups of water, add the chicken, and bring to a boil. Turn heat down and simmer chicken, checking every 15 minutes, and adding 1 cup of chile every time you check, until chicken is done. The fresh cornhusks give the chicken a most interesting and wonderful taste. You'll want to try this unusual recipe. It should serve 12, but it won't, because people will want more than one piece of chicken.

Red Chile Marinade

6 cups fresh red chile sauce
2 tsp. cumin
2 cloves garlic, minced
salt to taste
3 bay leaves
2 Tbsp. olive oil

Cook above ingredients for about 15 minutes over medium heat and let stand to cool.

Boil corn on the cob in a large pot for about 8 to 10 minutes. Serve chicken on several pieces of cornhusk, accompanied by the corn and a tossed salad. You can include beans and corn tortillas with the meal, if desired.

Arroz con Leche

Rice Pudding

1 cup uncooked rice
4 cups milk
2 sticks cinnamon
1 cup sugar (set aside 3 Tbsp.)
1 vanilla bean or 2 tsp. Mexican vanilla
4 eggs, separate yolks
1 cup raisins

Warm milk, and add vanilla bean and cinnamon sticks. Add rice, cover and cook over medium-low heat until done, about 15 minutes. Rice mixture will be somewhat liquid. Remove vanilla bean and cinnamon sticks, and add all but the 3 tablespoons of sugar. Turn to the lowest heat and stir in raisins and beaten egg yolks. In a separate bowl, beat egg whites until stiff, adding remaining 3 tablespoons sugar, one spoonful at a time until the beaten egg whites form peaks. Remove rice mixture from heat, fold in egg whites. Chill pudding until ready to serve.

❤ Abuelita made the most wonderful *arroz con leche*. It would heal any hurt.

❤ *Abuelito siempre le dijo a sus hijas, "Cojan una buena educación para por si les toca un mal marido, porque entonces se pueden mantener bien solas."*

Abuelito always told his daughters, "Get yourself a good education just in case you get a bad husband, because then, you'll always have your education to carry you through."

◆ When Abuelita would see a couple that didn't get along or weren't suited for each other, she would say, *"Mejor sola que mal acompañada,"* meaning, "Better alone than with a bad partner."

❤ My grandfather was a "soft touch." As a little girl, I would give him hugs and kisses, and he would say teasingly, "Get away. Don't be such a pest."

But I knew that he was kidding me, and that he actually loved all the attention that I gave him. He taught me a little children's song:

Naranja dulce, limón partido, dame un abrazo, por Dios te pido . . .	Sweet orange, sliced lemon, Give me a hug, I beg you for God's sake . . .
Si fuera falso tu juramento, en el momento te olvidaré.	If your pledge were false, I'll forget you in a minute.
Toca la marcha, mi pecho llora. Adiós señora, que ya me voy.	The march is sounding, my breast is weeping, Good-bye my lady, for I must go.
Si acaso muero en la batalla, tened cuidado de no llorar,	And, if I should die in battle, be careful not to weep,
Porque su llanto puede ser tanto, que hasta pudiera resucitar.	For your tears will be so many that I may end up being raised from the dead.

Spicy Spring

◆ *Caras vemos, corazones no sabemos.*
Faces we can see; what's in hearts, we don't know.
(You can't tell a book by its cover.)

❤ Abuelita served this dish when food was not plentiful, for it was a good way to make a few eggs go a long way. It is still one of my favorite breakfasts.

Tortillas con Huevos
Tortillas and Eggs

2 Tbsp. corn or olive oil
6 corn tortillas or four flour tortillas, torn or cut into 1-inch pieces
4 to 6 eggs, beaten
salt to taste

Heat the oil and sauté the tortilla pieces until golden brown. Add the beaten eggs, and cook, stirring the mixture in the pan until the eggs are firm. Tortillas and eggs can be eaten with salsa or ketchup. This is a dish to be creative with: add chiles, cheese, mushrooms, bacon, etc.

❤ Abuelita and Abuelito Contreras raised nine children: John, Gabe, Mike, Eddie, Gilbert, Willie, Margaret (my mother), Mercy (Mercedes), and Kathy. Kathy is a few years older than me, and we grew up as sisters. Some of my uncles are now in their eighties; only Uncle Willie has died.

When Abuelita was blue, she would sing, *"Las flores de mi jardín, llenas de tristeza y dolor . . . ."* (The flowers in my garden are filled with sadness and pain . . . .)

Actually, Abuelita's garden was beautifully filled with many kinds of flowers, especially roses of all colors. During World War II, she designated a rose for each of her sons serving in the war. The yellow was for Willie, red for Gabe, and Eddie's was pink. The yellow rose was always in trouble, and she hovered over it all the time, taking special care of it. All three uncles fought in many of the fierce battles in the South Pacific, and Uncles Eddie and Willie received Purple Heart medals. In the back yard, near the roses, we had a dome-shaped, cement niche, where San Francisco de Asís kept watch over our garden and my uncles. Abuelita frequently lit candles there and prayed. During the entire time that her sons served in the war, the candles were always lit.

Tacos de Atún

Tuna Tacos

12 corn tortillas
1 can water-packed tuna (save the water)
1 or 2 medium potatoes, peeled and boiled
2 green onions, finely chopped
8 large pimento-stuffed Spanish olives, finely sliced
¼ cup vegetable oil
½ head lettuce, shredded
taco sauce (See p. 63)

Break up potatoes, but leave lumpy, and add tuna with half of tuna juice. Toss in the onion and olives. Soften the corn tortillas in oil warmed to medium heat, and prepare one taco at a time as follows: Put about 2 tablespoons of the tuna mixture into a tortilla, roll it up (make a little cylinder), and secure it with a toothpick. When all the tacos have been filled this way, increase the heat in the skillet and quickly fry your tacos. Serve with shredded lettuce, cheese, and taco sauce.

♥ This is an easy dish to fix, and we would rush home after school to sink our teeth into these tacos. Tuna tacos were among the many meatless dishes Abuelita served during Lent. We ate no meat on Fridays, as was traditional among Catholics then.

Spicy Spring

◆ *Sobreaviso, no hay engaño.*
If you are forewarned, you cannot be deceived.

❀ *Azahar* (orange blossoms)
Steep orange blossoms to make a relaxing tea; good taken before bedtime.

❤ My grandparents often made the trip from Tucson to Nogales, Mexico, to buy vanilla, cheese, coffee, candy, corn tortillas, and even a little liquor. It was a long trip, and we traveled on the Old Nogales Highway, skirting the ranches along the Santa Cruz River, which flowed all the time in those days. On the way back home to Tucson, we would often stop and pick the watercress that grew wild alongside the river. That night for supper Abuelita would make a tomato and watercress salad to have with carne asada and the fresh corn tortillas that we had just purchased in Nogales.

Ensalada de Berro

Watercress Salad

3 cups cleaned, well-rinsed watercress, broken into pieces by hand
2 large tomatoes, thinly sliced
1 small red onion, cut into rings

Dressing

¼ cup vinegar
½ cup olive oil
salt and pepper to taste

Arrange items artfully on a platter and add dressing just before serving.

◆ *El que no oye consejo, no llega a viejo.*
He who doesn't listen to advice, will never reach old age.

♥ *El Tesoro*
   por Tía Kathy

Frente a la casa donde vivíamos había un paredón, el cual, para nosotros los niños, siempre nos parecía muy misterioso. ¿Que había al otro lado del paredón? Se rumoraba que habían esqueletos y joyas. Todos los niños le tenían miedo al paredón, y cuando teníamos que pasar cerca de allí de noche, siempre corríamos hasta nuestra casa.

Mi mamá siempre nos decía que había tesoro escondido en el solar donde vivíamos, y mi tío Jesús vino con un instrumento (un detector de metales) para buscar el tesoro, pero nunca halló nada. Mientras que él trabajaba, una multitud de niños lo seguía por dondequiera que iba. Aunque no encontró nada, sí que dejó una serie de hoyos por todo el patio.

The Treasure
by Aunt Kathy

In front of our house was a great adobe wall, and for us children, it was a very mysterious wall. What was on the other side? Some said there were skeletons and jewels. I think the children were afraid, and when we had to go near it after it turned dark, we would run home.

My mother always told us there was a treasure on the lot where we lived. My Uncle Jesús came with his searching instrument (a metal detector), and set out to find our treasure, but he never found anything. While he searched, a crowd of children followed him around. Although he didn't find treasure, he did leave several holes throughout the yard.

♥ My mother used to tell us kids that everyone has special powers, and we just needed to learn to develop them. She would play a game to help us develop our special powers, asking us to match colors without seeing them. She would assemble a set of colored Melmac dishes on the table, then blindfold us and give us a cup. We would feel the cup, and were to match it with the set of dishes of the same color on the table. After a little while, I could tell which ones matched merely by the feel. For some reason, I could *feel* the colors; the lighter colors felt different from the dark ones. I got to be very good at that game, but somehow over the years, I've lost that power. Maybe it's because I don't practice it anymore.

◆ *El uso hace el maestro.*
Practice makes perfect.

❤ I had a special bond with my grandmother, and it showed in many ways. Once, when I was about six, Abuelita lost her gold wedding ring. She and my grandfather had matching rings, with the other's name and the year they married inscribed inside the band. Abuelita lost that ring for about a year and was very upset about it. I was only six, but knew that it meant a lot to her. During that year, I dreamed three different times that the ring was among the roses that Abuelita always tended so carefully in the yard. Everyone just laughed at me and said, "She *didn't* leave her ring in the roses."

Later that year, a water pipe broke and they had to dig up the roses to get to it. The whole thing made a big mess of our yard, because they had to dig a long ditch all the way to street. Uncle Gabe came from California to help Uncle Mike and Abuelito dig it. When they turned up the rose bushes, there was the ring wrapped inside some roots!

Everyone made a big deal out of finding the ring in the roses like I'd dreamed, and Abuelita was so happy that she cried. Later, she remembered that they had dug holes to fertilize the roses the year before, and that must have been when she lost the ring. But I was a little girl and didn't know anything about fertilizing the roses. I figured those special powers that my mother taught me were at work in my dreams.

◆ *El que busca, encuentra.*
He who searches, will find.

◆ *Al que no habla, no se le oye.*
He who doesn't speak doesn't get heard.

SIMMERING SUMMER

Summer in Tucson is a time of refreshing rains, majestic purple-hued mountains, beautiful sunsets, and clear nights. And, of course, there is the shimmering, intense heat of more than 100°. Locals jokingly say, "but it's a dry heat," pointing out that the low humidity supposedly makes it feel less hot. Actually, the heat is quite tolerable for most people until the monsoon rains start, usually in July. Desert rains often appear as violent lightning storms, in a glorious upheaval of nature that quickly builds exquisite clouds, dumps life-giving rain, soothes the air, and cools the land.

When the storm ends, a local phenomenon occurs. The creosote bush, a desert plant with sprawling limbs and tiny leaves, releases a clean, robust fragrance that permeates the air with natural freshener.

The sunshine and sporadic rain work together to encourage the showy bougainvillea to spill its flamboyant flowers over adobe walls. A native of South America, this plant now flourishes around the world, wherever it gets the minimum in warmth and sunshine it requires. The Mexican Bird of Paradise livens the landscape with its flashy orange and red blossoms. Several other hardy plants bloom during this period, but most spend the summer trying to survive in this rugged land.

While many plants struggle under the sun, herbs and chile peppers grow eagerly in Tucson, given water and modest shade. Summer celebrations honor the cultures that have left their mark on the Tucson area—particularly Native American, Mexican, and Spanish.

Mexican food from Sonora reflects those cultures and their influence in this region. A specialty this time of year is the green corn tamal, made with fresh ground corn masa, green chiles, and cheese. Delicious!

Many Native American groups celebrate in the summer, featuring in their feasts some of the vegetables they introduced to the Spanish explorers—corn, chiles, and beans. These foods form the staples of Sonoran Mexican cuisine in southern Arizona and parts of northern Mexico.

Agua de Cebada
Barley Water

2 cups barley
3 cups sugar
1 lb. rice
1 stick cinnamon

Soak rice for 3 hours. Toast barley in a 350° oven until golden. Grind barley and rice together. Add 3 quarts water and enough sugar to sweeten. Strain out any solids. Vanilla optional.

Horchata
Rice Drink

4 cups rice
8 cups water
1 or 2 sticks cinnamon
2 cups sugar
6 oz. evaporated milk
2 Tbsp. vanilla

Soak rice and cinnamon sticks overnight in the water; next day, liquefy this mixture in a blender. Place in a 1 gallon container with sugar, evaporated milk, and vanilla, and blend well. Chill. Stir well before serving.

♥ Camberos Bakery was not too far from my regular path on the way to summer school at St. Augustine, a parochial elementary school. I would regularly stop and get a bag of doughnut holes for ten cents. At Thanksgiving time, the bakery would roast turkeys for families in the neighborhood for a small fee.

Bírria

Shredded Beef

4-5 lb. chuck roast or flank steak
2 bay leaves
2 large cloves garlic
1 can beer
2 jalapeños, seeds and veins removed
1 tsp. oregano
1 large onion, sliced

Put all ingredients into a Dutch oven or other heavy pan with a lid, and cook in oven at 300° for 4 to 6 hours. Beef is ready when it is so tender it falls apart when pulled with a fork. Put the meat in a bowl and shred it while it's still warm. Remove the bay leaves from the beef juice, and store in the refrigerator for a few hours until the fat congeals on the surface. Remove the congealed fat, then warm the remaining juice and serve as a light sauce to accompany your bírria.

This dish is usually served with Spanish rice (see p. 25), charro beans (see p. 93), finely shredded cabbage or lettuce, and tortillas of choice. Serves 8 to 12.

♥ This Mexican beef is often served at weddings. In preparation, my dad would dig a hole in the back yard, line it with rocks, and light a fire. Abuelita placed the meat with all its seasonings in a cast iron Dutch oven, and put the lid on firmly. When the coals were red hot and glowing, Dad would place the pan on the coals and cover the entire hole with a piece of tin. Then he would cover the tin lid with mud to seal it, and would leave the meat to cook overnight. Some of the old-timers would wrap the beef in banana leaves and wet burlap instead of using a Dutch oven.

❤ *El amor es un pasatiempo que pasa con el tiempo.*
Love is a pastime that passes with time.
Or, Love makes time pass, time makes love pass.

Ensalada de Frijoles Negros

Black Bean Salad

4 cups black beans (fresh-cooked or canned)
1 medium red onion, minced
1 medium red bell pepper, chopped
1 medium green bell pepper, chopped
4 large Roma tomatoes, chopped
1/8 cup cilantro, minced
¼ cup Mexican goat cheese or feta cheese

If using canned beans, rinse them before using. Put rinsed beans, onion, peppers, tomatoes, and cilantro in salad bowl. Crumble cheese into this mixture, and add vinaigrette dressing (see below). Toss and let the salad marinate an hour or so before serving. This dish is always better the next day.

Vinaigrette

½ cup olive oil
¼ cup vinegar
juice of 2 limes
salt, pepper to taste

Put all ingredients in a glass jar with a cover and shake well to mix.

*Cabrilla Frito**

Fried Cabrilla

1½ lb. Cabrilla fish
1 cup flour
1 egg yolk
2 egg whites
¼ cup olive oil
salt and pepper to taste

Rinse fish and pat dry with paper towel. In a large, flat dish, mix flour with salt and pepper, and set aside. Beat egg whites until stiff, and fold in 1 beaten egg yolk. Dip fish in egg mixture, then into flour mixture. Heat oil and cook pieces of fish until golden brown. Serve with lemon slices, tossed salad and steamed rice.

* Cabrilla is sea bass, which comes from the Sea of Cortés (also known as the Gulf of California), located between the Mexican state of Sonora on the mainland, and the peninsula of Baja California. Any firm white salt-water fish can be used for these recipes, but the results won't be quite as delicious.

◆ *No hay mal que por bien no venga.*
Nothing bad happens without some good coming out of it.

Caldo de Cabrilla
Cabrilla Soup

2 qts. water
2 large tomatoes, chopped
3 celery sticks, sliced thin
½ medium onion
4 carrots
1 lb. Cabrilla, cut into cubes
2 Tbsp. oil
1 bay leaf
1/8 cup cilantro, chopped
salt and pepper to taste

Put water and bay leaf in a medium-sized soup pot and start to heat. Put some of the oil in a frying pan, and sauté carrots and cilantro for three minutes. Add onion and tomatoes, and cook another three minutes. Add all these vegetables to the water that is heating. Wipe your skillet clean, add more oil, and sauté the fish, cooking until slightly firm. Add the fish to your vegetable broth, and cook on medium heat for another twenty minutes or so. Serve with lemon slices to squeeze over soup. I like my soup served over a ½ cup steamed rice.

Madeline, age 5, beside a lake near the Santa Cruz River in Tucson, 1950.

Carne Seca o Machaca
Dried Beef

Salt a chuck roast; make tiny cuts in the meat, and insert garlic cloves in the slits for additional flavor. (Abuelita inserted peppercorns and garlic for a flavorful, spicy, great-tasting meat.) Cook the roast, uncovered, in a 375° oven for 3½ to 4 hours, or until meat is crispy dry and brown. Cool the meat, then shred by hand. I cook the shredded meat with onion, green chiles, tomatoes, and cilantro in a skillet with a little corn oil.

This meat is the basic ingredient for carne seca and eggs (see p. 9), carne seca burritos and tacos, or cazuela (dried beef soup; see p. 114). This recipe is very good, but doesn't quite capture the flavor of the old-time carne seca that was dried in the sun. After it's made, carne seca can be stored in the freezer for year-round use. You'll find other recipes calling for carne seca throughout the book.

❤ Abuelito constructed a screened cage for making carne seca. The cage had wooden dowels inside for hanging the meat to dry. The screens helped protect the meat from animals and bugs.

Abuelita draped thin-sliced, salted steak over the dowels. Then, Abuelito hung the cage on the clothesline, and left it in the hot sun for several days. Some people set their cages on the roof, and one old restaurant in town, *El Charro,* still has a cage installed high on a pole. When the meat dried, it was dark red and didn't appear cooked. Abuelita then cooked the meat in the oven until it was brown. When that was done, she would pound the dried, cooked meat with garlic using a *metate y mano,* then she ground it by hand until the meat was tender and shredded.

◆ *El que viene tarde, atrás se queda.*
He who arrives late, will be last.

Darrell's Pargo a la Veracruzana
Darrell's Red Snapper Veracruz-style

1½ lbs. red snapper
¼ cup vegetable oil
½ cup flour
½ tsp. salt
2 large tomatoes, cubed
2 stalks celery, sliced
1 red bell pepper, cut into rings
1 green bell pepper, cut into rings
1 medium jar salsa

Put flour and salt in a plastic bag, then coat fish in this mixture. Heat oil in a large frying pan, add fish, and brown on both sides. Reduce heat to medium low, and add celery, tomatoes, peppers, and the jar of salsa. Cover and simmer for about 15 minutes. Serve over rice. Beautiful to look at, and also delicious!

◆ *De noche, todos los gatos son pardos.*
At night, all cats are gray.

Elote Frito

Sautéed Corn

1 Tbsp. olive oil
2 cups fresh corn kernels
½ onion
1 large tomato
salt and pepper to taste.

In a frying pan, warm your oil over medium heat, add corn, onion and tomatoes. Sauté until corn is done, about 10 to 15 minutes.

❤ Abuelita would only fry the white corn that is used to make green corn tamales. It has a sweet flavor and is a little firmer than other corn. You can use any fresh corn for this recipe, however.

❤ Abuelito would cut the corn off the cob for Abuelita, and she would fry it. Boy! Was it good! He'd always save the corn silk for medicinal purposes.

❀ *Barba de elote* (corn silk)
A tea made from corn silk is useful for minor urinary tract infections, burning sensation when urinating, and water retention.

Guacamole

2 large ripe avocados
½ cup onion, diced
¾ cup tomatoes, chopped
2 jalapeños, diced
¼ cup cilantro, chopped
juice of 2 limes
1 small clove garlic
salt to taste

Cut avocados in half, remove the pit, and peel the avocados. Mash pulp well with a fork, stir in diced onion, tomatoes, jalapeños, cilantro, and garlic. Squeeze juice of limes into mixture, and add salt to taste. Some people like to add a small amount of cottage cheese to their guacamole to make it go further.

I was six in this photo taken in 1951 in San Jose, California, during one of many visits to my parents. The visits were made possible by Abuelito's train pass as a railroad employee.

Guacamole de Papá

Dad's Guacamole

3 ripe avocados
½ medium onion, finely minced
2 Tbsp. cilantro, chopped
juice of ½ lemon
6 *güero* chiles*
1 clove garlic
9 *tomatillos,*** husks removed

Use a *molcajete* (see explanation with the following recipe) to mash your avocado, then place in a separate bowl. Add onion and cilantro to the avocado. Roast the chiles, then peel, remove the seeds and veins (See "The Great Chile Roast," p. 70), then grind them in the molcajete. Grind also the tomatillos and the garlic, and add to the mixture. Mix in the lemon juice. Add salt to taste.

*Güero chiles are yellow wax peppers, slightly larger than, and about as hot as, jalapeños. Some cooks use them interchangeably with jalapeños when they are available. Oh, and *güero* is what Mexicans call a blond person.

**Tomatillos are available fresh or canned. Fresh tomatillos resemble small green tomatoes with a brownish outer skin or dry husk that should always be removed before using them in a recipe.

Guacamole de Mamá

Mom's Guacamole

2 ripe avocados
1 clove garlic
3 güero chiles, broiled or roasted and peeled
2 Tbsp. cilantro
3 tomatillos, broiled and peeled
juice of 1 lemon
1 Tbsp. olive oil
2 tsp. salt (or to taste)

Grind garlic clove with the salt in a molcajete,* then add the chiles (peeled and seeds removed), and the tomatillos, and grind all ingredients together until desired consistency is reached. Add avocado and mash. Squeeze lemon over the mixture and serve.

**Molcajete*—a Mexican variation of the mortar and pestle. It is usually a crude small dish made from volcanic rock and standing on little legs. It is used for grinding ingredients for salsa and guacamole. The pestle part is called a *mano,* and is a round, hand-sized piece of the same stone. The molcajete must be "seasoned" by grinding dry rice and salt with it until its surface is smooth. Otherwise, bits of the volcanic stone will be ground into your food.

Jamaica

Hibiscus Tea

2 cup dried hibiscus blossoms
2½ quarts water
sugar to taste

Bring water to a boil and add your blossoms. Allow to cool. Strain and serve over ice with slices of lime on the glass. This is a beautiful summer tea.

Licuadas de Fruta

Fruit Smoothies

3 cups watermelon
1 cup ice
sugar to taste

Use watermelon or your favorite summer fruit to make this cool, refreshing drink.

❤ Abuelita always smelled of glycerin and rose water because she mixed rose water and a bit of glycerin to make her own moisturizer. She bought these items from *La Concha,* a drug store owned by the Dávila family, and located at the corner of Kennedy and Meyer Streets.

❀ *Rosa de Castilla* (tea rose)
Add fresh rose petals to beaten egg whites, and apply to the kidney area to cool and refresh. Steep petals in glycerin and water and apply to the face as a moisturizing cream.

To roast corn:

Soak the corn, husk and all, in water for a few minutes. Then put corn, still in the husk, on a very hot grill for about 20 minutes, turning frequently. Remove from the grill and let the ears cool, then pull back the husk, remove the corn silk, and serve.

Chile Mixture

½ cup chile powder
¼ cup salt

Mix together your favorite red chile powder and salt in a small bowl, and put the mixture into a shaker so you can sprinkle this wonderful flavor over your vegetables or fruit. And don't forget to use lime juice also! Lime juice sets the flavors and mingles a variety of tastes on your tongue.

In my grandparent's backyard, dressed for my first Holy Communion, in 1953.

Galletas de Bodas

Mexican Wedding Cookies

Traditionally served at weddings, but also made at Christmas time.

1 cup butter (or margarine) at room temperature
2 cups flour, sifted
½ cup powdered sugar, sifted
¼ tsp. salt
1 tsp. vanilla
1 cup pecans, finely chopped
1 additional cup powdered sugar, enough for rolling the cookies when they're done

Cream butter, powdered sugar, and vanilla until well blended. Add flour, salt, and nuts gradually to the creamed mixture and mix thoroughly. Divide the dough, and shape into two long rolls about 1¼ inches in diameter. Wrap in waxed paper and refrigerate several hours. Cut each roll into ¼-inch slices and place close together on an ungreased baking sheet. Bake in preheated oven at 350° for 15 to 20 minutes or until cookies are lightly browned on top. Remove cookies from the baking sheet and roll in powdered sugar immediately. Makes 4 dozen cookies.

❤ *Durante la Segunda Guerra Mundial, mis tíos Gabe y Eddie le mandaban el cheque que recibían por su servicio militar a mi abuelita, con instrucciones que ella lo usara para lo que ella necesitara. Pero, mi abuelita, por más que necesitaba el dinero, nunca lo usó, sino que lo depositó en el banco. Cuando regresaron del servicio militar, sus hijos quedaron muy sorprendidos cuando Abuelita les entregó su dinero.*

During World War II, both Uncle Gabe and Uncle Eddie sent their military paychecks home to my grandmother, telling her to use the money for whatever she needed. But, as much as Abuelita must have needed the money, she didn't cash the checks. Instead, she deposited them in bank accounts for her sons, and when they returned from the war, they were surprised to have little nest eggs waiting for them.

Margaret and Richard Gallego, Madeline's parents, on their wedding day, around 1944.

Simmering Summer

53

Gallego's snow cone stand, where we bought our *cimarronas* (snow cones) as children in the late '50s and early '60s.

♥ Abuelita had a little shelf in her bedroom that she used as an altar for the *Santo Niño de Atocha,* the Holy Child of Atocha, a saintly figure that originated in Atocha, a section of Madrid, Spain. According to the legend, when Spain was conquered by the Moors, only little children were allowed access to the Christian prisoners. Unexpectedly, a child, dressed in the clothing used by pilgrims in those days, appeared, and was allowed to enter a local prison with bread and

Abuelita's image (now in Madeline's possession) of *el Santo Niño de Atocha* patron saint of travelers, prisoners, and the sick. While her sons were serving in World War II, Abuelita considered the Holy Child as their special protector.

Salsa de Chiltepines *

Chiltepin Chile Sauce

1 Tbsp. *chiltepin* chiles (more or less)
4 large tomatoes
½ cup water
1 medium onion
2 tsp. olive oil
2 cloves garlic
salt to taste

Heat oil in skillet and toast chiles lightly until they are light brown and crisp. Remove from pan and sauté onion, garlic and tomatoes for 3 to 5 minutes. You can grind all ingredients by hand using a molcajete and mano, or you can put them a blender for a more liquid salsa. Add water until sauce reaches the desired consistency.

* Chiltepines are very small and very fiery peppers, which should be available in any store that carries Mexican food specialties. This is a good basic salsa, but you need to play around with it to see what your taste buds can handle, because this chile is *very* hot.

❀ When children had chicken pox, Abuelita would brown flour in a clean, dry pan. Then she would put the flour in a small muslin bag and rub it against the child's skin to help reduce the itching, and to help dry up the pox.

Salsa Fresca

Fresh Salsa

1 large red onion, minced
2 large tomatoes, chopped
juice of 2 limes
2 jalapeños, minced
2 Tbsp. cilantro, chopped
salt to taste

You may use a food chopper, but do not put the vegetables in the blender as that will liquefy them. Mix chopped onions, jalapeños, tomatoes, and cilantro. Add lime juice and salt to taste. Salsa's ready!

❤ In the summer, when we had a barbecue and made carne asada, we always fixed salsa fresca to spice up the meat.

❀ Aloe Vera

Aloe vera is a succulent that grows wild in the desert. Most people in Tucson have a few aloe vera plants growing in the corners of their yards, because they require such little care and are so useful. The juice of the plant is good for burns, including sunburn, and also for insect stings. You just break off a leaf and put the thick liquid directly onto your skin.

❀ *Manzanilla* (chamomile)

Manzanilla tea is good for stomach disorders, fever, or menstrual cramps.

Tacos de Varias Clases

A Variety of Tacos

Tacos de Carne

Beef Tacos

12 corn tortillas
1½ lbs. lean ground beef (add salt and pepper to taste)
¼ to ½ cup oil, but use only as little as needed
½ head lettuce, shredded
1 cup cheese of choice, shredded
taco sauce (See p. 63)

Place ¼ cup of seasoned, uncooked meat on half of a corn tortilla, then place it in a bit of warm oil over medium heat. When the tortilla is pliable, fold in half and cook until the tortilla is golden brown and the meat is cooked. Drain taco on paper towel. Open taco slightly and add lettuce, taco sauce and top with cheese. I usually make three tacos at a time, and continue the procedure until I've used up all my tortillas. This is the way Abuelita made tacos, and they're still the best! The kids always eat them all!

❀ Mesquite

This prolific tree populates the western United States. Add a couple of small green limbs or dried bean pods to your outdoor fire (or to your grill) to give a wonderful flavor to foods cooked there. Native Americans in the Arizona/Sonora border area boil the bean pods to make a great jelly. They also dry the seeds and grind them into flour for making bread.

Tacos Blandos

Soft Tacos

12 corn tortillas
1 lb. cooked, seasoned meat of choice (shredded beef, shrimp, chicken, etc.)
½ head lettuce, shredded
1 cup cheese of choice, shredded
taco sauce or salsa fresca

Put corn tortillas in a tortilla warmer or covered dish and heat them in a microwave on a low setting. Set all other ingredients on the table, and, when the tortillas are warm, fill with meat, lettuce, salsa and cheese. This is the way I make tacos now. They have fewer calories than the best (Abuelita's), and are almost as good.

❤ Our son Kevin's favorite birthday dinner request was always chicken tacos with taco salsa. He could consume a large number of these tacos.

Tacos de Pollo

Chicken Tacos
(a low-fat recipe)

Use 3 whole chicken breasts. Trim chicken breasts of skin and fat, then bake at 375° for 30 minutes or simmer in a skillet with 1½ cups of water for 20–30 minutes or until done. Save broth for Spanish rice. Cool cooked chicken and shred into a bowl, and add minced garlic, salt, and pepper.

Make one taco at a time and place in a pan for baking: Spray both sides of the corn tortilla with vegetable oil and heat tortilla briefly until pliable. Fill tortilla with a couple of tablespoons of chicken mixture, roll, and secure with toothpick. Place on a large baking sheet and repeat process until all tacos are made. Bake in a pre-heated oven at 375° for 20 to 30 minutes, or until they are crisp. Serve with lettuce, taco sauce and topped with cheese. Superb!

Salsa para Tacos

Taco Sauce

1 large can whole tomatoes
½ onion, minced
4 dried chiltepines chiles (see p. 59)
½ tsp. garlic salt or 1 clove garlic, finely chopped
½ tsp. oregano
salt to taste

Here's where the fun starts: Hand crush tomatoes into small bits. Mix all spices into the tomatoes. Rub the oregano between your palms and crush the dried peppers between your fingers as you drop them in. (Be careful not to touch your face or eyes until you have thoroughly cleaned your hands. Some people use rubber gloves, a piece of plastic wrap or a paper towel between their fingers to crush the chiles. Don't forget: it's the oil in the chile that causes the heat, and that oil is soluble, so, first, rub a bit of olive oil between your fingers, and then wash your hands with soapy water.) When all ingredients have been mixed well, salsa's ready! This is the only salsa I make with oregano, which gives it a distinctive taste, and we only use it on tacos and tostados.

❦ *Eucalipto* (eucalyptus)
A eucalyptus tea is good for flu and fever. Steep the leaves in water and inhale the steam to clear your nose and sinuses.

Tamales de Elote
Green Corn Tamales

2 doz. ears white sweet corn
2 cups shortening (or margarine)
2 Tbsp. baking powder
1 cup milk or cottage cheese to use as needed for moisture
2 cups green chiles, roasted, peeled, seeded, deveined, and cut into strips
1 lb. cheese of choice, cut into 1- × 2-in. pieces
salt to taste

Remove husks and silk from corn. Save the most tender husks to use as wrappers for the tamales. Cut corn kernels from cobs and coarse-blend in a blender or food processor. (Save corncobs and husks for use later in steaming the tamales.) Put the corn mixture in a bowl, and add shortening until it is well blended, then add baking powder and salt. If your corn masa appears dry, you may add, as necessary, milk or cottage cheese to moisten mixture.

Spread 2 Tbsp. masa on the broadest part of one husk. Place a few strips of green chile and one or two pieces of cheese on the dough, then roll the husk over the masa, from one side to the other, and fold down the top of the husk to cover the masa. To make a steamer, put about 4 cups of water in a deep pan, and then put in the reserved corncobs with the corn husks over them. Arrange your tamales so that the open part is facing upward, and steam them in a covered pot over medium heat for about 45 minutes.

You can also place your tamales in a conventional steamer to cook.

Simmering Summer

❤ Abuelito had peach and apricot trees, and several grapevines in the back yard. Every summer, when fruit was ripe and plentiful, he would make his famous *teswin*. Abuelito's wine was so strong, it would curl your toes. When the men in the neighborhood learned that his *teswin* was ready, they would come to visit and sit with Abuelito in the back yard under the mulberry tree for hours. Even after the wine season was over, friends would still come to Abuelito for his advice.

◆ *Amigo de buen tiempo, mudose con el viento.*
   A friend of good times changes with the wind.
   (Or: Fair weather friends are not worth having.)

Teswin
Corn/Barley Wine

3 lbs. dry corn
1 lb. barley
18 piloncillo cones (See p. 7)
6 gals. water
1 stick cinnamon
Add fruit of choice to ferment for flavor*

Toast corn and barley in oven until brown. Break corn by placing in a towel and hitting with a hammer. Do not grind. Place all ingredients in a 10-gal. earthenware crock, cover, and let stand 4 or 5 days. Strain the liquid through a cloth, and add more piloncillo and water to taste.

* You can use apples, apricots, pineapple, peaches, or any fruit that will ferment. The amount and the flavor depends on the maker, so you'll have to experiment. Start out with at least one pound of fruit or fruit mixture, and go from there.

❤ Abuelito cooked occasionally. He would make huge breakfasts for us on weekends: fried potatoes, pancakes, or eggs. He sometimes removed the husk wrapping the green corn tamales and fried the tamales in a large pan with butter until they were crisp on the outside; then, he would top them off with an egg over easy. He also made a type of bread that he called *pan ranchero* (ranch bread), which was very much like Irish soda bread. His *empañadas* with a spinach filling were a special treat.

Salsa de Tomatillos
Tomatillo Sauce

1 cup water
1 medium onion, chopped
2 fresh jalapeños, chopped, seeds removed if desired
1 clove garlic, chopped
2 Tbsp. chopped cilantro
1 lb. tomatillos, chopped

If using fresh tomatillos, remove brown husks. Put tomatillos into skillet with heated olive oil. Add onion, jalapeños, and garlic, and brown slightly. Put this mixture into blender with 1 cup water and cilantro, and blend lightly, but not to the liquid stage. Add salt to taste.

Tomatillos make a great sauce for fish; they can also be used in salsas or dips.

◆ Whenever unkind words were said about somebody, Abuelito would say, *"La zorra nunca ve su cola, por más larga que la tenga."* (The fox never sees his own tail, no matter how long it is.)

◆ Abuelito was a proud man; his word was his bond. To warn us not to dishonor our name, he would say: *"Quiero andar con la cabeza levantada y el sombrero alto."* (I want to be able to walk with my head up and my hat high.)

Tostadas

12 corn tortillas
3 cups pinto beans, cooked and mashed
1 cup cheese of choice, grated
2 cups taco salsa (see p. 63)
½ head lettuce, shredded
2 cups cooked meat of choice (optional)
½ cup oil

Fry the tortillas in oil until golden brown. Set them aside on paper towels until all are done. Spread beans evenly over each tortilla, then place a thin layer of meat (if desired), lettuce, taco salsa, and cheese. They make a magnificent dish!

Note: Tortillas can be crisped by spraying both sides with vegetable oil and placing 3 at a time in the microwave oven for about 3 minutes on high.

FLAVORS OF FALL

Summer pirouettes quietly, almost undetected, into autumn. Even when the temperature is still in the low 90s, the locals smile and say, "Yes, fall's in the air." Mesquite and cottonwood trees start to lose their yellowed leaves, and join the green-barked palo verde trees as beautiful, naked, outdoors wood sculptures.

Tucson loves fall, when the air is fresh and not too hot. People move outside again to hike, ride bikes, and gather for local fiestas. The serious bicycle racers travel in colorful packs of ten, fifteen, or more, over the hills and through the valleys, preparing for upcoming races.

Nights are cool, but days are sunny. This is the time for social and cultural celebrations featuring *música norteña,* northern Mexican dance tunes influenced by European rhythms and instruments. *Ballet folklórico* groups present Mexican folk dances, featuring ladies in colorful swirling skirts who dance flirtatiously around their partners. The intricate footwork, bright colors of the costumes, and the romantic nature of the dances are traditional. The Tohono O'odham Indians host evenings where they do another popular dancing style of the area called *waila* or "chicken scratch," which consists of the polka and two-step played on guitars, accordions, saxophones, and drums.

The harvest of fall is bountiful, and the small farms near Tucson welcome visitors to pick apples, pumpkins, okra, and other vegetables, as well as pistachios and pecans. Roadside stands offer fruits, vegetables, and chiles. Chile peppers are sovereign in the area, with their own special fiestas. The resplendent aroma of roasting chiles fills the air. Chile *ristras,* long strings of dried red chiles, hang everywhere, and even wreaths made of chiles are becoming popular. This is a time when the people are grateful for the land's bounty, and every celebration is opulent with superb food.

The Great Chile Roast

❤ One of the great pleasures of fall is the harvesting of chiles. Roasting makes peeling the chiles easier and releases their wonderful fragrance. Sometimes roasting is done outside. Often someone will set up a large tube-like grill in a supermarket parking lot and roast thirty-five pounds at a time for chile buyers. The air fills with the aroma of the roasting chiles, and people can't wait to get them home, so they can taste them.

Roasting chiles is done best over a hot mesquite fire. If you don't have enough mesquite wood, you can achieve good results by

Mary and Madeline picking green chiles in Hatch, New Mexico, 1983. They brought back 25 pounds of chiles that day!

throwing a few mesquite pods into an ordinary fire. Place chiles on a grill and char them on one side, then turn until all sides are charred and blistered. You can also roast chiles on a cookie sheet under the broiler in an oven. Place chiles in single files and roast under the broiler until their skin is blistered and a bit charred; turn chiles over and blister the other side. The blistering makes the skin of the chile separate from the "meat." Tomatoes, sweet and green bell peppers, and other chile peppers also can be roasted to make the peeling easier.

The reason for peeling chiles is that their skin is tough, rather than tender as the skin on a bell pepper; eating a bit of chile skin can be like chewing cellophane or plastic. To peel the chiles: remove them from the fire or the oven, place in a brown paper bag, and let them steam until they cool. The skins will start coming off as they cool. Abuelita would place her chiles on a damp kitchen towel and leave them until they cooled. Then, she would tenderly remove the charred, transparent skin. I often roast twenty-five pounds of green chiles at a time, and, after they cool, I quick-freeze them in freezer bags without peeling them. As I need the chiles, I pull them out of the freezer and place them under running water where the outer skin slips off easily. Then drain on paper towels. Chiles will keep frozen up to a year.

Diana Kennedy, in her book *The Cuisines of Mexico,* says that there are roughly 200 varieties of chile in the world, and that over a hundred of those can be found in Mexico. Many of those two hundred varieties are also grown in California, New Mexico, and Arizona. They are used fresh, dried, and in powder form, and they range from mild to *I'm-on-fire-but-this-is-so-good-I-can't-stop-eating-it!*

Chiles are an excellent source of vitamins A, C, and E. Used fresh, they contain twice the amount of vitamin C that citrus fruit has. The vitamin A content increases a hundred times as chiles ripen from green to red, and is not affected by cooking or freezing. Chiles are low in calories and sodium, and high in folic acid and potassium. Capsaicin, the ingredient in chiles that produces the heat, is known to be an effective treatment for shingles. Chiles release endorphins when eaten, producing a sense of well-being.

Never touch your face and eyes when handling chiles. When working with some varieties, it is best to wear gloves. The capsaicin in chiles is oil-soluble, and hand-washing with only soap and water alone does little to remove the burning ingredient. It is best to use a bit of vegetable oil on the affected area, then wash with soap.

Sopa de Albóndigas
Meatball Soup

1 stalk celery, sliced thin
2 carrots, sliced thin
1½ tsp. olive oil
2 qts. water
2 tomatoes, chopped or 1 can whole tomatoes, drained and chopped
1 lb. lean ground beef
½ cup uncooked white rice
1 egg, beaten
1 Tbsp. mint, chopped
1 large clove garlic, minced
1 tsp. salt (or to taste)

In a 4-quart soup pot, heat olive oil and sauté celery and carrots. Add water and bring this to a boil. In a bowl, mix beef, rice, tomatoes, garlic, onion, mint, and salt and blend well together with the egg. Form small meatballs and drop into the boiling pot. Turn heat to low and simmer for 45 minutes. Makes 6 servings. Serve with tortillas of choice (corn or flour).

Abuelita used ½ cup fresh masa with her hamburger meat instead of rice. This gave the meatballs a different and wonderful flavor and texture. I prefer this ingredient, but don't always have it on hand.

❤ Talking about albóndigas reminds me of Abuelita's mint. She kept it growing in a *tina,* or galvanized tub, beneath the outdoor water spigot, which dripped constantly. She used this spearmint, or *yerba buena,* in many dishes, including albóndigas, and as a remedy in tea. Abuelita shared her mint with her neighbors, who would ask, "Why is your mint always so nice?" They didn't realize that the drippy spigot kept Abuelita's mint green, hardy, and ready to use all the time.

❦ *Yerba buena or menta verde* (spearmint)
Spearmint tea is recommended for stomach discomforts. Abuelita made a weak tea for babies, and gave it to her children and grandchildren when they had colic. Put 3 or 4 fresh mint leaves in a cup of boiling water. Steep fifteen minutes or until tea has reached the strength you prefer.

◆ *Ayuda a tu prójimo.*
Help your neighbor.

♥ *San Martín Caballero* (St. Martin the Knight, or St. Martin of Tours) was Abuelita's kitchen saint. According to tradition, St. Martin was a soldier in the Roman army, who, when approached by a beggar who was hungry and cold, took his cloak, cut it in two, and gave half to the beggar. He is usually pictured on horseback, in the act of cutting his cloak with the sword, and giving it to the poor man on the ground. Abuelita kept a glass of water with a little bit of grass in it to provide for San Martín's horse. She always prayed over our food while she cooked, so we would always have plenty. And, although we didn't say a prayer out loud at the table, we were told that we should each, humbly and quietly, thank God for our food.

Oregano, *yerba buena* (mint), and aloe vera grow in a typical garden of the old neighborhood.

Arroz con Pollo
Chicken with Rice

4 lbs. chicken, cut in pieces and trimmed of all fat and skin
16 oz. can crushed tomatoes, with liquid
1 cup white rice
1 cup water
2 Tbsp. oil (corn or olive)
1 onion, minced
2 cloves garlic
1 bay leaf
½ tsp. pepper
½ cup diced green chiles
4 Tbsp. sherry, optional

Heat oil and brown chicken in a large skillet. Add sherry and cook down until most of the liquid has evaporated. Add all of the above ingredients to the chicken, cover and simmer 45 minutes. Add more liquid if necessary, but don't stir. Serves 6 to 8.

❤ When I was young, one of my favorite meals was roasted dove. Abuelito would go dove hunting and bring back about 15 or so of the scrawny little things. He prepared them by rubbing them with garlic, salt, and pepper, then he cooked them in a wood stove in our back yard over a mesquite fire. All those flavors baked into them until they were crisp. We loved this meal of roasted doves served with white rice and a salad of tomatoes and onions.

Besitos Mexicanos

Meringue Kisses

1½ oz. dark, semisweet chocolate
3 egg whites
¼ tsp. cinnamon
¼ tsp. cream of tartar
½ tsp. vanilla
¾ cup sugar

Heat oven to 350°, then turn off heat. While oven is heating, prepare this batter, so you can put the kisses into the oven shortly after it has been turned off.

Grate chocolate and set aside. Beat egg whites until stiff. Beat in cinnamon, vanilla, and cream of tartar, then add sugar, one tablespoon at a time until meringue is stiff and glossy. Stir in the chocolate. Drop a heaping tablespoon of the mixture on an ungreased Teflon cookie sheet or any other kind of pan lined with parchment paper, swirling each drop to a point. Place kisses in the oven for 3 hours without opening the door. When done, remove and store in an airtight container.

These kisses have a slightly brown hue from the chocolate, like wonderful little Mexican kisses. On occasion, I've made these a bit bigger than the recipe calls for and served them with a scoop of ice cream and a drizzle of chocolate syrup for a spectacular dessert.

Note: If you can find Mexican chocolate in your grocery store, omit the cinnamon listed among the ingredients.

Pollo en Mole
Chicken in Mole Sauce

1 tsp. olive or salad oil
1 onion, minced
2 cloves garlic, minced
¾ cup chicken broth
1 can (8 oz.) tomato sauce
¼ cup ground peanuts or peanut butter
1 Tbsp. chili powder
1 Tbsp. unsweetened cocoa powder
1 tsp. ground cinnamon
1 tsp. ground cumin
¼ tsp. black pepper
¼ tsp. cayenne
4 boneless, skinless chicken breast halves
3-4 prunes (liquefied in blender w/chili powder)

In a skillet, heat oil over medium high heat, and add onion and garlic. Cook, stirring, until onion is tinged brown; add 1 Tbsp. broth and stir in. Then, add tomato sauce, remaining broth, chili powder, cocoa, cinnamon, cumin, pepper, cayenne, and ground peanuts. Bring to a boil, reduce heat, cover, and simmer 10 minutes. Add chicken; continue to simmer until chicken is firm, about 15 minutes longer. Serve chicken breasts and sauce on rice with corn tortillas on the side.

Chilaquiles are versatile. They can be served at breakfast or brunch with eggs over easy on top, as a side dish with a main meal, or as the main course with beans, rice, and salad. My favorite way to eat them is for breakfast with eggs. You also may add your favorite meat to either recipe, if you desire.

Chilaquiles con Salsa de Chile Colorado
Red Chile Sauce Chilaquiles

2 Tbsp. oil
12 corn tortillas, cut into approx. 1-inch-sized pieces
½ white onion, finely chopped
2 cloves garlic, minced
2 cups red chile sauce (See p. 56)
1 cup cheddar cheese
1 to 1½ cups chicken broth
⅛ cup green olives, chopped
2 green onions, chopped

Heat oil in skillet and sauté tortilla pieces slightly. Add garlic and onion and cook a bit more. Add the broth, chile sauce, olives, and ¾ cup of cheese, and simmer 12 minutes. Garnish with green onions and the rest of the cheese.

❤ Abuelita always added a small amount of vinegar to her red chile sauce. She believed it rounded off and balanced the flavors.

Flavors of Fall

♥ *Muchas de las casas en la Calle Main tenían pequeños nichos sobre las puertas, donde las familias tenía un santo de su devoción. Una vez le pregunté a Abuelita sobre esta costumbre, y ella me contó que se originó durante el tiempo de la Prohibición, para indicar a la gente que pasaba por la calle si había licor o no. Cuando el santo tenía una velita prendida, esa era la señal de que se podía comprar licor en esa casa.*

Many of the homes on Main Street had little niches or small alcoves, built into the exterior walls above the doorways, where the residents usually had the image of a favorite saint. When I asked Abuelita about the custom, she told me it dated back to the days of Prohibition, and served to indicate to passersby whether there was liquor available or not. When the image of the *santo* had a burning candle in front of it, that was a signal that you could get liquor at that house.

This house on Main Street, across from the grandparents' house, has a little *nicho* containing the image of a saint above the entrance. During prohibition, a lit candle in the nicho advertised whether there was liquor for sale in the house.

Empañadas de Calabaza

Pumpkin Turnovers

Filling

3 cups cooked fresh pumpkin
½ tsp. salt
¼ tsp. ground cloves
¼ tsp. ground nutmeg
¾ cup brown sugar

Bring all above items to a boil, then turn the heat to its lowest setting, and simmer for about 10 minutes, stirring frequently. Set aside to cool.

Dough

2 cups flour
½ tsp. salt
2/3 cup shortening
6 Tbsp. water

Sugar Mixture

½ tsp. cinnamon
¼ cup sugar

1 egg, beaten, for glazing the finished empañadas

Cut shortening into salted flour until you have pea-sized pieces. Add water to make a dough. Divide dough into 10 or 12 small balls. Roll out the balls to make small, flat circles. Place the filling on one half of the circle, fold the other half over it, and press the edges together with a fork to seal them. Prick the tops of the empañadas with a fork several times (to vent steam during baking), and brush them with the egg for a glaze. Bake at 350° for about 20 to 30 minutes, or until golden brown. While they are still warm, dip the empañadas in the sugar mixture. Serve warm.

❤ Uncle Willie believed in natural herbs and good health. Every morning before breakfast he ate five garlic cloves, claiming that they would ward off colds and help with his blood circulation.

He was the neatest person in the family, and tried to teach us to be neat as well. He also taught us kids that we should help those that needed help.

In later years, when Abuelita started to lose her eyesight, she would start sewing projects and not be able to finish them. Uncle Willie would come to her house and clean it, mop her floors, and run errands. If he found any of her unfinished sewing projects, he would sit down at the sewing machine and finish them for her.

Chiles Güeritos en Adobo
Marinated "Güerito" Chiles

1 lb. güero (yellow) chiles
(See note with guacamole recipes p. 45.)
¾ cup olive oil
½ cup lemon juice
1½ tsp. salt, or to taste

Roast and peel chiles, and remove the seeds, but retain the stems on them. Marinate chiles in olive oil mixture 24 hours and serve as hors d'oeuvres or condiments. Stem is preserved to hold the chile while you're eating it.

❤ Abuelito encouraged our family to play *Lotería,* a Bingo-like game, because he thought it brought the family together. We played with picture cards that were named in Spanish after the picture on them, like *gallo* (rooster) and *sirena* (mermaid). We used dried pinto beans as the markers.

While we had these fun family evenings, Abuelito would make popcorn for us with an old wire contraption that he held over an open fire or over the gas flame on the stove. He was willing to try new things, such as different foods, unlike Abuelita, who preferred for things to stay the same.

❤ *La Marchanta*
   por Tía Kathy

Cuando éramos niños, mi mamá le compraba tortillas a una señora india que mi mamá llamaba simplemente "La Marchanta." Para mí y para los demás niños se nos hacía muy curiosos el nombre de esta señora.

Ella era una mujer alta y delgadita. Tenía una voz muy bajita, y, cuando hablaba, hablaba muy despacito. Su vestuario era interesante: siempre usaba un blusa de un material brilloso y una falda larga de colores muy vivos y alegres. En su cabeza traía un canasto lleno de tortillas recién hechas, y cuando llegaba a la puerta, tocaba muy levemente.

Los años pasaron, y luego no vimos más a la marchanta. ¿Quién sabe que le pasaría?

The Merchant
by Aunt Kathy

When we were children, my mother would buy tortillas from an Indian lady whom she simply called "The Merchant." For me and for the rest of the children, her name seemed very curious.

She was a tall, thin lady. She had a voice that was very low, and, when she spoke, she would speak very softly. Her dress was interesting. She wore a blouse made of some shiny material, and a long skirt of colors that were very alive and happy. On her head she carried a basket filled with freshly-made tortillas. When she came to the door, she would knock lightly.

The years passed and afterwards we no longer saw "The Merchant." Who knows what happened to her?

◆ *Ladrón que roba a ladrón, tiene cien años de perdón.*
A thief who steals from another thief has one hundred years' pardon.

Carne a la Mexicana
Mexican Beef

One 4-5 lb. chuck roast
1½ lbs. fresh tomatoes, crushed
   (or 1 28-oz. can crushed tomatoes)
1 cup fresh green chiles
   (or 1 8-oz. can green chiles)
¼ cup chopped cilantro
1 large onion, minced
2 cloves garlic, minced
salt and pepper to taste

Place all ingredients in large pan and cook covered in oven at 300° for about 6 hours. The meat is done when it easily shreds off with fork. Shred meat completely. Serves 8 to 12.

This beef is excellent in a flour tortilla as a burrito or soft taco. It also stands alone well as a main dish with side dishes of rice and beans, or a large salad and calabacitas.

❤ *Cuando mi Tío Miguel tenia cinco años, la familia vivía en Calabasas, cerca de Tubac, como a unas 50 millas al sur de Tucson. En ese tiempo, los húngaros (así llamaban a los gitanos en esos días) caminaban por esta parte del país y a veces hacían campamento a las orillas del Río Santa Cruz cerca de Tucson.*

Un día cuando Tío Miguel iba de camino a la escuela con otros niños, vinieron unos húngaros a caballo y se lo robaron como por una semana. Abuelito juntó un grupo de rancheros vecinos, y fueron en busca del niño. Llevaban sus pistolas, y fueron a caballo hasta el campamento de los húngaros y lo rescataron. El niño dijo que no lo habían maltratado. La familia nunca supo porqué se lo llevaron.

Cuando yo era niña, los húngaros a veces venían a Tucson y hacían su campamento en la parte sur de la ciudad. Mi abuelita les tenía mucho temor úporque ya se habían robado a su hijo en años pasados. Cuando se rumoraba que habían húngaros en el vecindario, le ponía candado a las puertas y no me dejaba salir. Ella decía: "No dejen que miren a la Nekita, porque se la van a robar." De ese modo yo crecí también teniéndole temor a los húngaros.

Uncle Gilbert serenades us after dinner, around 1978.

Flavors of Fall

When my Uncle Mike was about five years old, the family lived at Calabasas, near Tubac, some 50 miles south of Tucson. In those days, gypsies, whom we called *los húngaros* (the Hungarians), would travel around this part of the country and occasionally set up camp along the Santa Cruz River near Tucson.

One day, when Uncle Mike was walking to school with other kids, gypsies on horseback came by and swept him up, kidnapping him for about a week. Abuelito gathered a group of men, who took their guns, went on horseback into the gypsy camp and rescued him. He claims that he wasn't mistreated, and the family never knew why he was taken.

When I was a little girl, *los húngaros* would come into Tucson and set up camp on the south side of town. Because of her son's kidnapping, Abuelita was afraid of the gypsies. Whenever she heard rumors of gypsies in the neighborhood, she would lock the doors and wouldn't let me out of the house, saying, "Don't let them see *Nekita*, because they'll steal her!" So I also grew up with a fear of the gypsies.

In San Jose, California, late '40s: Aunt Kathy and Aunt Mercy pose in Uncle Gabe's car, while little Elaine, Aunt Mercy's daughter, climbs on the back.

Encaje Mexicano

Mexican Lace Cookies

1 cup flour
1 cup finely chopped nuts
½ cup butter
½ cup Karo light syrup
2/3 cup brown sugar, packed down

Filling

1 cup whipped cream
3 Tbsp. powdered sugar
1 tsp. instant coffee
½ tsp. cinnamon
melted sweet chocolate–optional

Preheat oven to 325°. Line baking sheet with aluminum foil, generously greased. In a small bowl, mix together flour and nuts; set aside. Melt butter in a small saucepan. Stir in corn syrup and sugar, and bring to a boil. Remove from heat and add flour mixture. Drop dough by rounded teaspoonfuls onto the greased foil at least 3 inches apart. Bake 8 to 10 minutes.

Cookies appear bubbly or lacy when done. Let cookies cool slightly on pan 1 or 2 minutes. Then, working quickly because the cookies harden while cooling, remove cookies with a spatula, turn them onto wax paper, and roll each one to form a cone.

Dip the rim of the cones in melted sweet chocolate, then fill the cones with sweet cream.

❀ *Canela* (cinnamon)
Crush cinnamon sticks and make a tea. Use the tea to settle an upset stomach, or to help reduce postpartum bleeding.

Pan de Elote
Mexican Spoon Bread

3 eggs
1/3 cup oil
1 cup corn meal
½ tsp. soda
¾ cup milk
1 can creamed corn
1 cup cheddar cheese
½ cup cottage cheese
4 oz. diced green chiles
1 tsp. salt

Beat eggs slightly. Add milk, oil, and creamed corn, and mix together. Add corn meal, soda, cottage cheese, and salt. Pour half the mixture into a greased casserole. Spread chiles and half of the grated cheese over this. Pour the other half of the mixture on top. Cover with remaining cheese. Bake 45 minutes at 400°. Serves 6 to 8.

Pastel de Gallina
Chicken Pie

6 corn tortillas
1 cup cooked chicken, cubed
1 cup cheese (longhorn or Monterey Jack), grated
½ cup roasted, chopped green chiles or
    1 small can green chiles, chopped
1½ cups 2% milk
1 whole egg plus 4 egg whites
2 Tbsp. oil
salt and pepper to taste

Warm oil in skillet and dip corn tortillas in oil to soften them. Line a 9 in. pie plate with five tortillas. Put cubed chicken, half the cheese, and half the green chiles on top of the tortillas. In a small bowl, mix beaten eggs, milk, salt, and pepper, then pour this mixture on top of chicken and tortillas. Place the sixth tortilla on top, and add the remaining green chiles and cheese. (The result is like a quiche with a cover.) Bake in a 350° oven for 40 minutes, or until the mixture sets.

◆ *Caso juzgado, caso cerrado.*
Case that has been judged, case closed.

Frijoles Pintos
Pinto Beans

4 cups dried pinto beans
3 qts. water
2 ham hocks
1 onion

Clean and rinse beans. Put into a large pot with water, ham hocks, and the whole onion. Bring to a boil, then turn heat down to simmer for about 3 hours. Add more water if necessary. Salt to taste.

Hint: 1 cup of dried beans produces 2 cups of beans when cooked.

Since my family loves beans, I double the beans and water, but not the ham or onion.

Frijoles Charros
Charro Beans

pinto beans, cooked as in recipe above
1 large white onion, diced
3 large tomatoes, chopped
3 large garlic cloves, minced
5 or 6 serrano chiles, seeds and veins removed, chopped
1 cup cilantro, chopped
8 slices of bacon

Cut bacon into tiny pieces, and cook, but not too crisp. Add onion, tomatoes, garlic, and chiles, and cook for about 5 minutes. Add this mixture to the cooked beans, and cook another 30 minutes. Salt to taste. Garnish with cilantro.

Frijoles Refritos
Refried Beans

Nowadays, refried beans are no longer fried in lard, as Abuelita did, but are placed in a skillet and crushed with a potato masher. Add either some of the bean juice or milk to the beans to make them the consistency you want, and top with cheese of your choice before serving.

◆ *Los de muy alto, grandes caídas se dan.*
Those who climb the highest, fall the hardest.

Madeline's mom, Margaret, and Aunt Kathy trying to learn one of Uncle Eddie's soft-shoe routines about 1962.

Flavors of Fall

These two dishes are wonderfully exciting and have a completely different taste. You must try them both! *Pipián* is a sauce made with ground nuts, seeds, and spices.

Pollo en Pipián con Chile Colorado
Chicken Pipián with Red Chile

4 chicken breasts
2 cups water
2 cup red chile sauce
1 cup pumpkin seeds *(pepitas)*
1 tsp. olive oil
1 clove garlic, minced
salt to taste

Put the 2 cups of water in a pan over medium heat, add chicken breasts, and cook until chicken is done. Set aside chicken to cool; reserve the broth. Remove skin and bones, cube chicken, and set aside. Roast seeds in the oil over medium heat until slightly golden. (If you can find pumpkin seeds already roasted, you can save yourself this step.) Cool and grind in a blender. To the pan you used to roast your pumpkin seeds, add garlic, chicken, red chile, broth, and pumpkin seeds. Cook for 30 minutes over medium low heat. Add salt to taste.

Pollo en Pipián con Chile Verde
Chicken Pipián with Green Chile

4 chicken breasts
1 clove garlic
1 cup green chiles
1½ cup tomatillos
1 medium onion, sliced in circles
1 cup shelled pistachios
2 Tbsp. cilantro, chopped
salt to taste

Place chicken breasts in a glass baking dish. Cover with foil and bake at 350° for half an hour. In a skillet, slightly roast your pistachios in oil and set aside. Put a medium glass container with water, tomatillos, garlic, green chiles, cilantro, and salt in the microwave. Cook for 4 minutes at high power. Put mixture in a blender with pistachios and blend until well mixed. Place onion slice on each chicken breast, pour blended mixture over chicken and bake another ½ hour.

Most pipián recipes call for a sauce made with ground pistachios, pumpkin seeds, or other nuts. This one is different.

Pipián de la Familia Ochoa
Ochoa Family's Pipián

- 1 can evaporated milk
- 2 15 oz. cans green beans, drained (save the juice in case you need it for thinning the sauce)
- 2 cups fresh chile sauce or 1 can Las Palmas (or any other available brand) red chile sauce
- 2 Tbsp. oil

Heat oil gently and blend in 2 Tbsp. flour. Stir in the can of milk, mix until smooth, and bring mixture almost to a boil, salt to taste. Add chile sauce to the milk mixture, stir until smooth, and bring to a boil. Add drained green beans. Keep warm over very low heat until ready to serve.

This is one of those dishes that is even better the second day, so doubling the recipe to have some left over for later in the week is a smart thing to do.

❤ Betty Ochoa, a member of one of Tucson's founding families, gave me this recipe many years ago. It was handed down from her grandmother. Betty made this simple dish a culinary delight for guests by serving it elegantly in a silver chafing dish.

Caldo de Queso

Potato-Cheese Soup

6 large potatoes, peeled and cubed
1 medium to large onion, chopped
l large clove garlic
1 Tbsp. olive oil
3 to 4 fresh green chiles, peeled, seeded, and chopped
    (enough for ¾ cup) or one 6-oz. can chopped chiles
½ lb. shredded cheddar cheese
½ qt. chicken broth and ½ qt. milk, or ½ qt. milk,
    ½ qt. water, and 2 chicken bouillon cubes
cilantro for garnish, optional

Sauté potatoes, garlic, and onion in oil in a large soup pot. Cover ingredients with liquid, and simmer until tender, about 30 minutes. Toward end of the cooking time, add chiles. When serving, add a handful of cheese (to taste) to each bowl. Abuelita would add the cheese to the soup before serving, and let it melt in the soup. It can be done either way.

❀ *Ajo* (garlic)

Today, many devotees take garlic in the form of odorless tablets, but Abuelita used garlic in its natural form for a number of ailments, including lowering both blood pressure and blood sugar. Steep 6 cloves in 2 cups boiling water, and drink to relieve constipation. Steep crushed garlic cloves in warmed honey for a couple of days, and take a teaspoon or two for a dry, hacking cough. Garlic is also supposed to promote growth if rubbed on the fingernails.

Salpicón

Cold Dinner Salad

4 medium potatoes, boiled, then peeled and sliced
6 carrots, peeled, then boiled and sliced
1 can whole beets, drained and sliced (or already-sliced canned beets)
1 can green beans, drained
1 can garbanzos, drained
6 hardboiled eggs, sliced (optional)
1 bay leaf
1 garlic clove
1 tsp. oregano
1 cooked beef tongue, skinned and sliced or 1 flank steak, about 3 lbs.
2 large white onions, thinly sliced
1 cup red wine vinegar
½ cup salad oil
salt and pepper to taste

Cook meat in 2 quarts of water with salt, bay leaf, garlic and oregano for approximately 2 hours. Slice meat thinly and return it to the water to soak up some of the broth for 1 hour. In a different dish, marinate onions in vinegar, oil, salt, and pepper.

Layer the meat and the vegetables (except for the onions) in a casserole dish. Top with the onions and egg slices, then pour the vinegar mixture over the whole thing. Refrigerate several hours, until cool. Serves a large crowd, 12 to 16 people.

❦ *Cebolla* (onion)

Steep thin slices of onion in honey for an hour, and take a teaspoonful of that honey as needed for colds, cough, and congestion of the lungs.

❀ *Papas* (potatoes)
When we had the mumps, Abuelita sliced potatoes very thin and placed the cool slices on our cheeks. It probably didn't check the swelling, but made us feel cool and better.

❤ For serving, Abuelita would place a warm corn tortilla on a dinner plate, then arrange lettuce on the tortilla, and top it with salpicón. She would usually serve this dish when we had special visitors. When I was young, I liked the way the beets tinted the potatoes such a beautiful magenta color. I loved everything about this dish except the garbanzos, which I would carefully pick out and push to the side.

Enchiladas Sonoreñas

Sonoran Flat Enchiladas

Tortillas

2 lbs. fresh masa*
½ cup cottage cheese or cheese of choice
½ tsp. baking powder
1 tsp. salt
1 cup water (approximately)
½ cup vegetable oil for frying the tortillas

Into a large bowl, mix the first four ingredients in the order listed. Add water slowly, one tablespoon at a time until the masa sticks together in a ball. Take a 2-inch ball of dough, place it between two pieces of plastic wrap, and flatten to form a small, round tortilla. Set the tortillas on a moist cloth until you have them all made. Heat oil in a skillet, and very carefully cook each tortilla in the hot oil, lightly browning on both sides. Place tortillas on paper towels to drain.

(recipe continued on next page)

Dip your fried tortilla in the chile sauce, then place it on a plate. Put a handful of shredded lettuce on the tortilla and spoon the topping over it. If you like chile sauce, add more. Serves 6.

Topping

½ cup green olives, chopped small
½ cup green onions, chopped
1 cup Mexican enchilada cheese, crumbled (also called *queso fresco* or white Mexican cheese)

Mix all ingredients together in a bowl.

Additional ingredients

3 cups (or more) red chile sauce, warmed (See p. 56)
½ head shredded lettuce

* The fresh masa referred to here and elsewhere in the book is the kind of freshly prepared masa that one can purchase at a tortilla factory, and the same masa that is used for making corn tortillas and tamales (See pp. 132–37), made from corn that has been soaked in lime, then ground. In many stores that carry Mexican food specialties, you can buy an instant masa mix (under names like *Masa Harina* and others) that can be prepared according to the directions on the package and used in these recipes. The taste, however, won't be as pleasing and flavorful.

❤ When Abuelita made tamales, she would save some masa for these enchiladas, which are the only type of enchiladas she ever made. She made her own tortillas, and her own red chile sauce from the ristra. These enchiladas are my favorites.

Sopaipillas

2 cups flour
1 Tbsp. vegetable shortening
1½ tsp. baking powder
1 tsp. salt
1 Tbsp. sugar (optional)
1 cup milk
1½ cups vegetable oil for frying

Mix all dry ingredients and cut in shortening. Add milk a little bit at a time until dough can be handled easily. Form into 2-inch balls, and let the dough rest for 30 minutes. Roll out each ball on well-floured surface to form small tortillas. Fry each one in hot vegetable oil in a deep pan. To test if the oil has reached the right temperature, toss a tiny pinch of dough into the pan. If it floats and sizzles, the oil is hot enough.

Carefully place each sopaipilla in the oil, turning it until it browns and puffs up. (Frying will create a pocket of air in the middle.) This process should only take a few minutes for each one. As they are done, remove sopaipillas from the oil and place on paper towels to drain. The sopaipilla may be used as a bread. Some people like to bite off a small corner and fill the cavity with honey. Others coat them with powdered sugar while still warm.

Sopaipillas can be made in triangles, little square pillow shapes, or whatever strikes your fancy. You can quarter the dough after it has had a chance to rest, roll it out, and cut it into pie-shaped pieces, or into squares. If you omit the sugar in the ingredients above, you can use this recipe to make fry bread to serve with beans or your favorite meat.

❤ Abuelito had a lot of patience, and he often made things with me. One afternoon, we made paste from flour and water, then took newspapers, wood, and string, and he helped me make a little kite. We cut strips of cloth from an old dress of mine and made a long, colorful tail, and we had a great time all afternoon flying it in a nearby field. Of course, it was special to me because we had done it all together.

Relleno para Pavo (Guajolote) o Pollo
Stuffing for Turkey or Chicken

1½ loaves French bread
1 tsp. poultry seasoning
4 potatoes, chopped
1 lb. ground beef
½ cup green onions, chopped
1 cup chopped celery
½ cup raisins (optional)
¼ cup green olives
1½ cups turkey broth (made by boiling giblets and neck)
¼ lb. butter
3 apples
1 tsp. poultry seasoning
salt to taste

Slice bread, butter it, toast it, then cube it, and set aside. Cook ground beef about 12 minutes; add chopped potatoes for the last 6 minutes of cooking time. Add this meat and potato mixture to the bread. Dice apples, chop green onions and celery, and add to the above mixture. Add raisins and poultry seasoning, and just enough broth until the dressing is moist enough to hold together for stuffing. Salt to taste. Don't forget to allow extra baking time if you cook the stuffing inside the bird. (See recipe p. 80 for corn bread dressing.) This stuffing, with its wonderful mixture of flavors, is almost a meal in itself.

♥ Thanksgiving is not a traditional Hispanic celebration, so at my grandmother's house, we didn't observe this holiday until years later. Abuelita would stuff several roasting chickens with this mixture and cook them.

The food preparation for a holiday meal was always a great deal of fun, with Abuelita giving assignments to everyone for peeling, chopping, and cutting. While we worked, we would tell jokes, and laugh, and have a great time, and it seemed that we finished the chores quicker with everyone there.

Caldo de Tortilla
Tortilla Soup

8 corn tortillas, cut into thin strips
1 Tbsp. olive oil
2 large tomatoes, chopped
3 cloves garlic, minced
2 large, cooked chicken breasts, skinned, deboned, and cubed
6 to 8 cups of chicken stock
1 cup whole corn kernels
¼ cup cilantro
4 green onions, chopped
1 large, mild jalapeño, minced (optional)

Bake corn tortilla strips on a cookie sheet at 350° until lightly browned; set aside. In a large soup pot, heat olive oil over medium heat, and sauté garlic, tomatoes, chicken breasts, cilantro, and green onions about 4 minutes. Then add the corn, and cook another 2 minutes. Add chicken stock, and cook 15 minutes. In last 5 minutes of cooking time, add the jalapeño, if you dare. Top soup with browned tortilla strips. You'll have great soup in no longer than 30 minutes.

Flavors of Fall

❤ Abuelita would peel the pomegranate's tough, brown skin and give my cousin Elaine and me the sweet seeds. She would save the skins and steep them to make a tea-like mixture. Then she would rinse her white hair in this liquid to stain it darker. She would laugh and say, "One day I'll paint my hair blue, like the rich ladies do!"

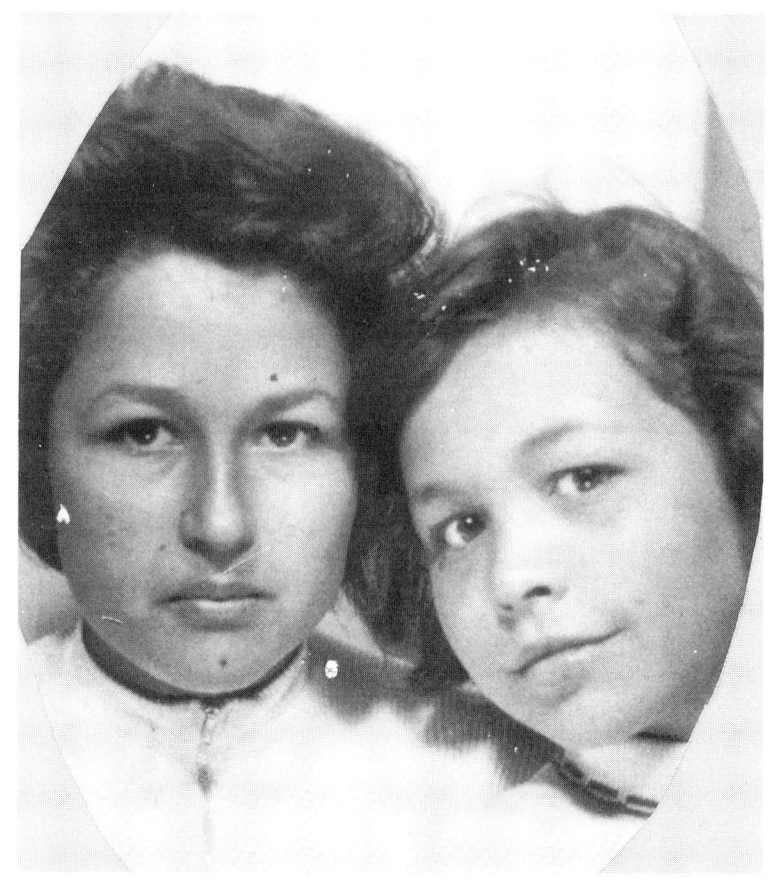

My cousin Elaine, Aunt Mercy's daughter, and me after movies at the Fox Theater on Congress Street about 1955.

WINTER COMFORTS

The winter season brings cooler weather to Tucson, and sometimes rain accompanies the storms that sweep down from the northwest coast in waves. Storms create a welcome crispness to the air, but the sun soon warms the days. The holidays are bright and sunny, and even if snow falls on the Old Pueblo, as it does occasionally, it generally melts by noon.

During Christmas week, *Las Posadas* depicts the journey of Mary and Joseph seeking shelter for the night when the birth of her child is pending. *Los Peregrinos,* as those depicting the Holy Family are called, are accompanied through the neighborhood by a large group of people, singing as they travel along asking for shelter at each house. Traditionally, they are turned away at every location, and continue on their journey until they reach a designated house that finally grants them admission. *Pan dulce* (sweet bread), *bizcochuelos* (cookies), and Mexican hot cocoa are generously passed around at the closing of the event.

Tamales are traditionally served on Christmas Eve. They are a dish that requires quite a bit of preparation, so families and friends gather to make them in the weeks or days prior to Christmas.

Luminarias, tiny lights or candles set into brown paper bags weighed down with sand, line our driveways and flat roof tops with a distinctive Southwestern touch. In recent years, people even dress the saguaros in tiny white fiesta lights (cool, so they don't harm the plant's tender skin) to show off the unique shapes of the tall cacti. Winter is a fun, festive time filled with celebration and good food.

Bizcochuelos
Christmas Cookies

1 cup shortening
2 eggs
1¼ cups white sugar
½ cup cornmeal
1½ cups all-purpose flour
1½ tsp. baking soda
5 Tbsp. anise seeds
1 Tbsp. ground cinnamon
¼ cup orange juice

Blend shortening and sugar, then add eggs. In another bowl, combine cornmeal, flour, baking soda, anise seeds, and cinnamon. Mix well. Add dry ingredients slowly to the wet mixture and blend as you go. Then add orange juice. To make the cookies, take a walnut-sized piece of the dough and roll it between your palms to make a rope about 5 inches long. Form a circle with the rope and overlap the ends. Bake at 350° for 8 to 10 minutes.

❤ This is generally a Christmas cookie, but is also used for any special gathering, such as baptisms, first communions, and confirmations. After the baptism ceremony, the families usually return to the home of one of the family members to continue the celebration with fun and food. Traditionally, the infant's godfather calls all the young children to gather around him. His pockets are overflowing with change, and he generously tosses it to the children, who scramble for the money, squealing with delight. This tradition is called *tirar el bolo,* and is supposedly done to assure prosperity for his godchild.

❤*La Fe*
por Tía Kathy

Cuando alguien tenía problemas severos, o cuando ella o algún miembro de la familia se encontraba en una situación muy dificultosa para resolver, mi mamá siempre hacía sus oraciones a Dios. La fe que teniá en eso tiempo, cuando la vida era a veces muy dura, cuando tenían muchos niños que criar, era la única salvación de ella, de su esposo, y de su familia. Mi mamá rezaba tanto al acostarse como también al despertarse por la mañana. Cuando yo era niña, también veía que Mamá oraba durante el día mientras hacía su trabajo, en voz muy leve, casi como un murmullo.

Yo por eso soy muy espiritual, porque siempre me recuerdo de mi Mamá y sus oraciones. Esta fe fue uno de los mejores regalos que nos dejaron nuestros padres. Todos mis hermanos y hermanas también tienen mucha fe; sin ella no sé que nos haríamos.

Faith
by Aunt Kathy

When someone had difficult problems, or when she or some other member of the family faced situations that were hard to resolve, Mama would pray to God. The faith she had in those times, when life was sometimes much harder, and when they had a lot of children to raise, seemed to be the only thing that kept her, her husband, and our family afloat. Mama would say her prayers both at bedtime and upon arising in the morning. When I was a child, I also saw Mama praying as she did her work during the day, in a soft voice, almost like a murmur.

That's why I'm a very spiritual person, because I always remember my mama and her prayers. This was one of the best gifts our parents left with us. All my brothers and sisters also have very strong faith; without it, I don't know what we would do.

Buñuelos

Fritters

2 cups flour
1 tsp. baking powder
1 tsp. sugar
1 Tbsp. shortening (or margarine)
1 cup milk
oil for deep-frying

Combine all dry ingredients with the shortening and mix well. Add half the milk, and mix with your hands. Add the rest of the milk, a little at a time until you can handle the dough without it sticking to your fingers. Knead it on a floured board. Form little balls, about 2 inches around, then roll them flat with a rolling pin and deep fry in very hot oil. Serve with this syrup:

Syrup

1 lb. piloncillo* or 2 cups brown sugar
1 cup water
whole peel of 2 oranges
2 cinnamon sticks
2 whole cloves

Bring all ingredients to a boil and simmer until the mixture thickens slightly. Strain to remove the orange peels, cinnamon sticks, and cloves, and serve over the buñuelos.

* See note, page 7.

Winter Comforts

♥ We usually ate buñuelos on Christmas Eve, the same evening we traditionally made tamales. The women worked in the kitchen making the tamales, while the men sat outside talking, drinking beer, smoking, and stirring the menudo, a beef tripe soup, which cooked in a big cast iron pot on a wood-burning stove. Abuelita started the syrup for the buñuelos early in the day, so the house filled with the wonderful aroma of the spices. When she was finished making the syrup, she made candied orange peel out of the peel she had used for the syrup.

Later, we went to the *Misa de Gallo* or Midnight Mass, then came home to open our presents. We weren't allowed to eat meat because the day was a Holy Day of Obligation, but, after Mass, we could eat all the tamales we wanted.

Christmas Day was filled with visits from neighbors and friends, who brought plates of their best Christmas cookies. They stayed to enjoy Abuelita's wonderful tamales and coffee. Or some might have a shot of tequila with Abuelito.

Christmas of 1965: brothers David (in striped shirt) and Richard, ages 8 and 12; sister Joanne, 10; and cousin Lucy, Aunt Mercy's youngest daughter, 12, at our grandparents' home in Tucson.

Café con Kahlúa

Coffee with Kahlúa

1 oz. Kahlúa liqueur
½ oz. tequila
hot coffee
whipped cream
cocoa powder

Make a pot of good Mexican coffee and pour into cups. To each cup, add 1 oz. Kahlúa and ½ oz. tequila. Top with whipped cream and add a dusting of cocoa powder.

❤ When I think of tequila I think of Olga's Cafe, a little place in Nogales, Sonora. Regardless of what you order to eat there, they first serve you homemade salsa and freshly made tortilla corn chips with fresh Mexican cheese sprinkled on top, and shooters of tequila with slices of lime. Olga's is always a stop on our shopping trip to Nogales, a good way to prepare us for the bartering style of shopping in that little border town.

◆ *No te vayas queriendo.*
Don't leave wanting.

❤ Once when Mary, my co-author and one of my best friends, and I were in Spain, she was admiring a beautiful hand-painted vase at an open-air market. She was hesitant to buy it, and had just about decided to wait until some other time. Pushing to make the sale, the elderly Spanish lady who tended the pottery stall said to her, *"¡No te vayas queriendo!"* meaning, "Don't leave wanting (the vase)!" Mary immediately decided to take the vase, knowing she might not return and would probably later regret not buying it in the first place.

Now, when we shop together, we tease each other with, *"¡No te vayas queriendo!"* and it helps us make the decision to get what we want so we won't regret it later!

Cajeta
Caramel Sauce

12 cups milk
2½ tsp. cornstarch
½ tsp. baking soda
3 cups sugar
1 stick cinnamon

Place cornstarch and baking soda in a bowl, and stir to dissolve with 2 cups of the milk. Put the remaining 10 cups of the milk in a large, heavy-bottomed saucepan, and bring to a boil. Add the milk with cornstarch and baking soda, and stir. Then add the sugar and cinnamon, stirring the mixture with a wooden spoon as it cooks for about 1 hour, or until it holds together, so that you can see the bottom of the pan as you stir. Cool and pour into jars you can cover. Makes 6 cups. Great warmed and served over ice cream, or eaten just as it is with a spoon.

❤ When we were kids, going across the border to Nogales, Mexico, from our home in Tucson, was always an exciting adventure. We all wanted to go because it was a chance to shop in another country, where the store owners were willing to barter, and where, when you bought something, there was always an air of delight.

If, for some reason, we kids didn't get to go to Nogales with Abuelito, he would bring us this candy as a special treat. It still comes in little round wooden boxes, along with small wooden spoons for eating. The place of origin of this candy is listed on the lid as Celaya, Guanajuato, Mexico, where my dad was born.

Cazuela de Carne Seca

Carne Seca Soup

1 Tbsp. olive oil
2 cups carne seca (See p. 41)
½ onion, diced
2 garlic cloves, minced
2 medium tomatoes, peeled and chopped
4 large potatoes, peeled and cubed
¼ cup cilantro, chopped
½ cup green chiles, cut into stripes
salt to taste

In a large 4- to 6-quart pot over medium heat, sauté onion and garlic in oil for about a minute. Add chopped tomatoes and cook until mixture starts to boil. Add carne seca, potatoes, green chiles, and cilantro, along with 2 quarts water, and bring to a boil. (If your chiles are hot, add them at the end of the cooking time so your soup doesn't get too hot.) Turn heat to simmer, and cook about 30 minutes or until potatoes are tender. Add more water if you like a thinner soup, since potatoes tend to absorb water in cooking. Salt to taste, and serve with tortillas of your choice, corn or flour.

❤ To explain why we sometimes pray to a particular saint, Abuelita would say that sometimes you need a mediator to speak on your behalf, and, since the saints were on a different plane from us, being closer to God, they probably would be heard better.

Papas con Chorizo
Potatoes with Chorizo

Cook chorizo lightly in a skillet. Drain most of the fat. Peel and chop potatoes into small pieces, and add them to the chorizo, cooking them until golden brown. Drain any extra fat, and serve with fried eggs on the side, if desired.

Macarrones con Chorizo
Macaroni with Chorizo

Boil macaroni according to package directions. Drain, and put in a greased casserole. Mix in some fried and drained chorizo, one 8-oz. can of tomato sauce, and 1 cup grated cheese of your choice. Bake at 350° for 20 minutes, or until cheese is melted. Excellent with a tossed salad and refried beans.

❤ Our son Cliff would run with his father, Darrell, in 5K fun runs a few years ago. I'm sure he did it for the chorizo and eggs they enjoyed after the run at Micha's Restaurant in Tucson, rather than for the exercise.

Cochitos
Ginger Cookies (pig-shaped)

5 cups flour
1 tsp. salt
1 tsp. baking powder
1 tsp. baking soda
1 tsp. cinnamon
3 Tbsp. ginger
⅛ tsp. nutmeg (dash)
½ tsp. cloves
1 cup shortening (or margarine)
1 cup brown sugar
¾ cup granulated sugar
½ cup coffee
2 tsp. vanilla
½ cup dark molasses

Mix first 8 ingredients. In a different bowl, cream shortening and sugars. Mix coffee and vanilla with molasses to thin, then add to shortening mixture. Combine dry and wet ingredients and form a dough. Chill the dough a couple of hours, then roll thin. Cut cookies with a cookie cutter shaped like a pig, which is traditional, and place on greased cookie sheet. Bake at 350° for 15 minutes. Makes 2 dozen cookies.

❤ My first real job was in Burbank the summer my cousin, a friend, and I moved to California. I was the only one of the three to get a job, so it was imperative that I work. When the manager at Penney's Department Store asked me if I had experience in alterations, I answered, "Of course."

Actually, I knew nothing about altering men's suits, which was the first thing I was given to do. I didn't know you measured for the pant's cuff from the crotch down. I measured from the waist, and produced a very nice Bermuda suit.

The manager came and spoke to me, but, after my sad story about how much we needed the money from this job, he asked me to dinner instead of firing me. Eventually, I did learn to alter, but was never very good at it.

Enchiladas

12 corn tortillas
½ cup oil (corn or olive)
¼ cup black or green olives
½ cup green onions, chopped
1½ cups grated cheese of choice
3 cups chile sauce (See p. 56)
½ head lettuce, shredded finely

Mix together the olives, onions, and cheese. Heat a couple of teaspoons of oil in a pan, and carefully dip a tortilla in it for a few seconds, then turn the tortilla over, and heat the other side. Do this to soften all the tortillas so they will be pliable for rolling. In the meantime, warm your chile sauce (and don't forget to sprinkle it with a little vinegar). Spread a small amount of sauce on the bottom of a baking dish. Place two tablespoons of the olives, green onions, and cheese mixture on one side of a tortilla. Then roll, placing seam-down on dish. Do this until all tortillas are filled. Top with the chile sauce, the remaining filling mixture, and the rest of your cheese. Bake at 350° for 30 minutes. Top with shredded lettuce and serve.

This is a basic enchilada recipe that is my favorite. But if you wish, go crazy, as with the tacos, and fill them with eggplant, mushrooms, cooked spinach, crab meat, or whatever you like.

Cocido
Vegetable Beef Soup

Make a beef stock of the following, and cook 2 hours:

3 lbs. beef soup bones (joint bones, short ribs, or oxtails)
3 qts. water
3 cloves garlic, cut in half
1 large onion, cut in half

Skim off the foam, and cool several hours in refrigerator; remove any fat that hardens on top and discard. If using bones, remove them, but if you use ribs or oxtails, leave them in, and serve them as part of your soup.

To this stock, add:

1 small head cabbage, chopped
2 medium zucchini squash, sliced
2 large tomatoes, chopped
2 large potatoes, quartered and sliced thick
2 celery stalks, sliced thin
2 whole ears of corn, cut into 1½ inch rounds
¼ lb. fresh green beans, cut in 1½ inch pieces
1 cup garbanzos (Abuelita added garbanzos, which I always promptly removed from my plate. Since I don't like them, I usually don't put them in my cocido.)

Add all the vegetables to the broth and bring to a boil. Turn heat down and simmer for 2 hours. Garnish with chopped, fresh cilantro, and serve with pieces of lime to squeeze on the soup.

❀ Abuelita thought that soup bones with marrow were the best for soup and for your joints. She said they helped with arthritis.

❤ When we were young and picky about our food, Abuelito told us a story of a mean stepmother who frequently cooked beef soup.

Mexican Fudge

12 oz. semisweet chocolate chips
8 oz. milk chocolate chips
¼ tsp. salt
1 cup chopped nuts (your choice)
1 tsp. vanilla
1 tsp. instant coffee
1 tsp. cinnamon
1 can condensed milk

Line an 8 × 9 in. pan with waxed paper. In a heavy, medium-sized saucepan, over low heat, melt chocolate chips together with condensed milk, salt, instant coffee, and cinnamon. Stir until well-blended. Remove from heat, and add nuts and vanilla, mixing well. Pour into a 9 in. square pan, and cool in refrigerator until firm.

❤ When Abuelito asked, "Wanna go to California?" my answer was always, "Oh, yes! When do we leave?"

Since my grandfather worked for the railroad, we got free train passes. It was not unusual for Abuelito, Aunt Kathy, and me to hop on the train, go to San Jose to visit my parents and Uncle Gabe for a couple of days, then turn around and come back home. Abuelita required more time to plan and a longer stay, so she usually didn't go with us. But I was always ready. One time, Abuelito got off the train at a stop to buy us hamburgers, and the train went off and left him. He had to wait until the next day to catch a train to Tucson, but I had a wonderful time traveling back home, because I knew all the stops and the working crew.

Pollo Borracho
"Drunken" Chicken

1 large cooking chicken, cleaned and cut into pieces
1 can tomato sauce
1 can cola soft drink
1 can beer
1 small package raisins
¼ cup green olives, not pitted
½ onion
2 cloves garlic
4 large potatoes, peeled and cubed
2 large stalks celery, chopped
4 carrots, peeled and sliced
2 bay leaves
1 Tbsp. oil (olive or corn)
steamed rice for serving (See p. 26)

Heat oil in a large pot and sauté chicken pieces 10 minutes. Put in carrots, celery, and potatoes, and cook 5 minutes more. Add onion and garlic, and cook another 3 minutes. Pour all liquid into pot and bring to a boil. Turn heat down to simmer, and cook covered for 30 minutes. Uncover, add all other ingredients, and simmer another 45 minutes, adding the bay leaves for the last 15 minutes. Serve over steamed rice.

Rompope
Rum Eggnog

4 eggs
¾ cup rum
1 can (14 oz.) condensed milk
½ tsp. cinnamon
1 tsp. vanilla extract

Mix in blender and serve chilled with dash of cinnamon. The rum cuts some of the thickness, but it is a wonderfully festive drink. Must be refrigerated.

❀ *El Tiradito,* meaning "the little castaway," is a shrine located near my neighborhood at the edge of a barrio known as *El Hoyo,* or "The Hole." This Mexican American neighborhood was built outside the south wall of the old Spanish Presidio that established the city of Tucson.

As a child I heard several versions of the story of *El Tiradito,* but they all include a tragic murder within a family at the site. The shrine was built around 1870 or 1880 in Spanish mission style with an altar for candles to honor *el alma perdido,* and people started lighting candles for the lost soul. It became a place, especially during hard times like the Great Depression or *La Crisis,* for desperate people seeking miracles to light candles and pray.

Since *El Tiradito* was within walking distance of our house, my friends and I would often light candles as teenagers, but not for *el alma perdido* or seeking a healing miracle. At that time, we were far more interested in boys with dreamy brown eyes, and we prayed that they would ask us to the dance or to one of the house parties that were so popular at that time.

In the late '50s and early '60s, I never feared walking the barrio at night. A group of us would walk to Gallego's for our *cimarronas,* or snow cones, in the evenings. We never dared to do anything wrong because our neighborhood was a gathering place in the evenings for the *viejitos,* or older ones, who sat outside and visited and also kept watchful eyes on what the young people were doing. Today, it is a different story.

In the 1970s, most of the houses in *El Hoyo* were destroyed for progress—the Tucson Convention Center and a huge parking lot. But the shrine of *El Tiradito* was preserved and people still light candles there today.

El Tiradito, with candles lit at the shrine. Grandson, Dalton, age 1 in 1998, is playing in the foreground.

Winter Comforts

Sopita de Fideos
Vermicelli Soup

1 Tbsp. olive oil
1 lb. fideos (vermicelli), broken into 1-inch pieces
1 small can tomato sauce
½ onion, chopped
2 small cloves garlic, minced
1 Tbsp. chopped cilantro
1 qt. chicken stock or
1 qt. water with 2 chicken bouillon cubes

In a 2-quart pan, heat oil over medium fire. Add fideos and brown until most of pasta is golden. Add chopped garlic and onion; cook slightly. Add tomato sauce and chicken stock. Cook until pasta is softened. Add cilantro just a few minutes before serving. Salt and pepper to taste.

Old friend, Guayo Moreno, seated between *mis abuelitos* at the kitchen table. He only came to visit every two or three years, but was always welcomed with a bowl of soup.

◆ *Camarón que se duerme, se lo lleva la corriente.*
The current sweeps away the shrimp that goes to sleep.

Sopa de Viejo
Old Man's Soup

6 flour tortillas, cut into 1 inch pieces
1 large onion, diced
2 cloves garlic, minced
½ cup fresh roasted green chiles, cut into strips
1 cup Monterey Jack cheese
½ qt. chicken broth
½ qt. milk
1 Tbsp. oil
salt to taste

Heat oil in a 2-quart pan. Add tortilla pieces and brown lightly, about 4 minutes. Add onion and garlic; cook 3 more minutes. Then add the chicken broth and milk, and cook over medium heat for 30 minutes. Add green chiles and cheese. Cook 3 more minutes. Serves 4 to 6. This was one of Abuelito's favorite soups.

❤ Abuelito was a great storyteller, and he especially loved keeping us up with ghost stories on hot summer nights, when we kids were sleeping outside on cots. He told us about *La Llorona* (The Crying One), a woman whose children died in a fire when she left them alone to go to a party, and the story called "Dancing with the Devil at Elysean Grove" about a girl who disobeyed her parents and went dancing, only to discover that her partner was the devil. There are a variety of versions of these stories. Abuelito kept us in anticipation for days, as he told little bits of *Aladino y la Lamparita Maravillosa* (Aladdin and the Magic Lamp) each night until it was finished.

After I graduated from high school, my cousin Elaine, a friend, and I went to California to make our fortunes. We returned home after three months, flat broke, and willing to seek our fortunes in Tucson, instead. On the night of our return, Elaine and I decided to go to a local dance to catch up on everything we'd missed that summer. When we got home that night, Abuelito unlocked the door for us, and then hid around the corner with a sheet over his head to scare us, like he had done when we were kids. Later that night, he passed away, leaving us with sweet memories of the loving, tender man that he was.

Abuelito, around 67, in front of his prized grapevine-covered ramada in 1960.

Tamales Dulces

Sweet Bean Tamales

3 cups freshly cooked pinto beans, drained
    reserve ½ cup bean juice
1 cup piloncillo or panocha*
½ cup water
1/3 cup oil
1 tsp. cloves
1½ tsp. cinnamon
½ cup raisins

In a large frying pan, warm oil and add the beans and the bean juice, and mash them together with a potato masher right in the pan. Cook them about 10 minutes, then add the cloves and cinnamon. Dissolve the piloncillo or panocha in 1/2 cup of water in a small pan on the stove, or in a bowl in the microwave. Add this to the beans, and cook down most of the liquid. Add raisins and your filling is ready for making your tamales.

Masa

3 lbs. masa as for tamales
1 cup margarine
½ cup water
1 tsp. baking powder
1 tsp. salt

Follow preparation instructions on page 136.

*See note page 6.

❤ During the holidays, Abuelita made sweet bean tamales with pinto beans, sugar, and spices. She would serve them to the adults with coffee, and to the children with a glass of milk or Postum. Her sweet tamales were small and wrapped like pieces of hard candy, with the filling in the middle, and bows tied at each end with strips of cornhusks.

Tamal Perdido
"Lost" Tamal

> 3 lbs. prepared masa (See p. 136)
> 4 cups prepared carne con chile (See p. 135)
> ½ cup green olives
> ½ cup raisins (optional)

Use a greased 9 × 13 in. baking dish, or a casserole of equivalent size. Spread half your masa evenly on the bottom of the pan or dish. Layer with the 4 cups carne con chile, green olives, and raisins, and top with the remainder of the masa. Bake about 45 minutes at 350°. Serve with beans and a salad.

❤ Abuelita began early to get ready for the making of tamales the day before Christmas Eve. She rendered large pieces of fat on a wood stove in the back yard, and used the fat in flavoring the masa. We ate some of the cracklings from the fat with fresh flour tortillas. My, how we loved those wonderful tortillas and cracklings with homemade salsa! The days of making tamales in this manner are long gone, and only the sweet memories remain.

❤ Fifteen years ago, I began meeting with a close group of ten friends who wanted to learn to make tamales. We had such a good time together, and made such nice tamales, that we decided to continue the next year, and the next, and every year after that. Nowadays, we get together for a day sometime before Christmas and turn this time-consuming task into a party, producing a large number of fine tamales, and having a great time doing it. We share the work and the costs: everyone has an assigned item to bring. We have even deviated from our traditional beef and pork by making turkey, chicken, elk, or veggie tamales.

The tamal-making party ends with a tamal-eating party that evening. Everyone brings a dish to go with the tamales: green salad, pinto beans, Spanish rice, dessert, and margaritas or Mexican beer to drink. This is now our yearly custom, so the tradition of making tamales will not be lost.

The tamales are finished; we're ready to eat! Left to right: Toni Saccani, Darrell Thorpe, Jerry Freund, Mary Engels, Sally Freund, Madeline Thorpe, Roger Engels. Tino Saccani is taking the photo.

Tamales

First, you make

Carne con Chile
Meat with Chile

4 lbs. of your meat of choice (beef or pork roasts), cut into large cubes (I mix beef and pork for my tamales)
2 Tbsp. oil
2 large cloves garlic
3 Tbsp. flour
4 cups fresh red chile sauce (dry, canned, frozen, or chile paste)
salt to taste
green olives (optional, to be added at time of assembling the tamales)
jalapeños (optional)
raisins (optional)

Put meat in a large pot with water to cover, salt, and garlic over medium-high heat. When the water comes to a boil, turn heat down, and simmer until meat is tender. Let the meat cool, and shred. Strain the meat broth and save for mixing masa. In a large frying pan, heat the shortening, add flour, and brown lightly. Add the shredded meat, chile, and enough broth to bring to the desired thickness. Simmer all about 15 minutes, and set aside to cool. While you're waiting for the meat mixture to cool, prepare the masa.

(Recipe continues on next page.)

Masa para Tamales
Masa for Tamales

5 lbs. fresh prepared masa, or the equivalent in masa harina mix
2½ cups shortening (Abuelita used lard; I use margarine)
2½ tsp. baking powder
2 tsp. salt, or to taste
2 lbs. corn husks, soaked, rinsed, and drained (see below)

Stir salt and baking powder into the masa, and mix shortening in. (I always add a bit of chile to give some color to my masa.) Blend well with your hands, adding some of the reserved strained meat broth to bring it to the desired texture. Mix the masa until a tiny ball of it floats when dropped in a glass of water.

Small bundles of dried corn husks can be bought in stores that carry Mexican food specialties. The husks must be rinsed to remove leftover bits of silk and any dirt, and soaked in water for a few hours to make them pliable again. Drain when you're ready to assemble the tamales, so they will still be moist and pliable.

To assemble the tamales:

Spread 2 to 3 tablespoons of masa on the broadest part of the husk. Place 2 tablespoons of carne con chile in the center of the masa. Add an olive for special flavor. Some people add a strip or two of canned or pickled jalapeños. (If I make them for myself, I always make a few with a teaspoon of raisins in each, as Abuelita made them. This is the way I prefer them.)

Roll the husk lengthwise around the tamal, and fold the top down. Put tamales in a steamer, or in a pot whose bottom you have lined with extra husks. Put the open end of the tamales facing up; keep adding them in layers as you make them. Add 4 cups of water to the pot and bring to a boil. Turn heat to low, and simmer for about 30 to 45 minutes.

This recipe makes 4 to 5 dozen tamales, depending on how thick or thin you spread the masa.

Full Circle

❤ Near the end of her life, when she was in her eighties, Abuelita was almost completely blind. To cheer her up, and to remind her of the beautiful flowers she always grew in her gardens, I gave her a rose.

"Oh, mi'ja (mi hija, my daughter)" she said. "It smells wonderful. It is so beautiful. *Gracias."*

"Abuelita," I answered, "I'm sorry you can't see how beautiful it is."

"But I've seen roses, and I remember," she reminded me. "Gather your good memories while you're young, so when you get old, you can bring them all back."

Now I'm the abuelita. My grandchildren call me Nonie.

❤ Last year, when we celebrated my husband's birthday, I was in charge of the kitchen, as my grandmother had always done. For dinner and the celebrations that evening, we had our five sons and their wives and girlfriends, eleven grandchildren, Opal (my husband's mother, who was eighty-five years old at the time, but has since passed away), two sets of in-laws, and several other family members; thirty-one people in all. I took great pleasure in being able to feed our large family, one that always eats *con mucho gusto* (with great relish). Here is what I served:

Birthday Menu:

Chiltepin salsa
Guacamole
Corn chips
Marinated and grilled chicken
Marinated and grilled steak
Salsa fresca
Pinto beans with ham hocks
Spanish rice
Flour tortillas

Condiments:

Shredded lettuce, chopped tomatoes, grated cheese

Dessert:

Pastel de chocolate

We were happy to have most of the children spend the night at our house. Eight grandchildren played games and had a great time together. We let them stay up as long as they wanted, and they slept all over the floor. The next morning, they woke up to the cinnamony aroma of French toast being prepared by our eldest son, Jesse, as his father has always done on weekends for our boys.

❤ *Hijo de gato, gatito.*
Like father, like son.

Just like my grandparents did with their family, we are gathering our fine memories surrounded by our families and friends, all united by the love of good food.

Full Circle

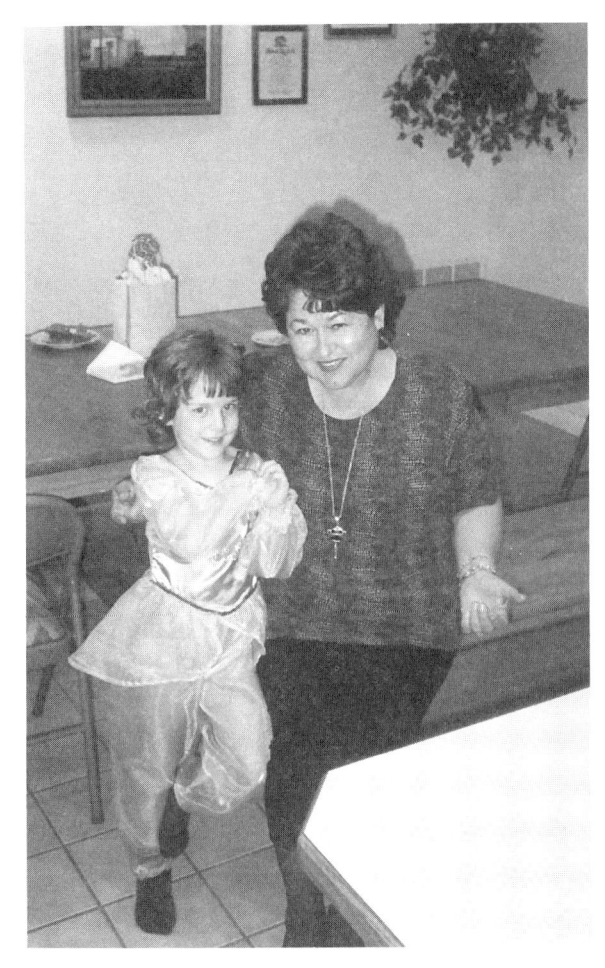

Abuelita Madeline and granddaughter McKenna Thorpe, age 4, in 1998. McKenna is wearing her Halloween costume of Disney's "Jasmine."

◆ *Como te miras, yo me miré.*
Como me miro, tú te mirarás.
The way you look, I used to look.
The way I look, you will look.

INDEX

A

Abuelita's Jericalla, 15
Agua de Cebada, 34
Arroz Blanco al Vapor, 26
Arroz con Leche, 23
Arroz con Pollo, 75
Arroz Mexicano, 25

B

Barley Water, 34
Beef Tacos, 61
Besitos Mexicanos, 76
Bírria, 35
Bizcochuelos, 108
Black Bean Salad, 36
Bread Pudding, 6
Buñuelos, 110

C

Cabrilla Frito, 37
Cabrilla Soup, 38
Café con Kahlúa/Tequila, 112
Cajeta, 113
Calabacitas, 40
Caldo de Cabrilla, 38
Caldo de Chile Verde con Maíz, 122
Caldo de Queso, 98
Caldo de Tortilla, 104
Capirotada, 6
Caramel Sauce, 113
Carne a la Mexicana, 85
Carne Asada, 8
Carne con Chile, 135
Carne Seca con Huevos, 9
Carne Seca o Machaca, 41
Carne Seca Soup, 114
Cazuela de Carne Seca, 114
Champurro, 115
Charro Beans, 93
Chicken in Mole Sauce, 77
Chicken Pipián with Red Chile, 95
Chicken in Red Chile, 12
Chicken Pie, 92
Chicken Pipián with Green Chile, 96
Chicken with Rice, 75
Chilaquiles con Salsa de Chile Colorado, 78
Chilaquiles con Salsa de Chile Verde, 79
Chile Colorado, 56
Chile Mixture, 48
Chile Verde, 57

Chiles Güeritos en Adobo, 83
Chiltepines Chile Sauce, 59
Chocolate Cake, 21
Chorizo, 116, 117
Christmas Cookies, 108
Cochitos, 118
Cocido de Chile Verde, 124
Coffee with Kahlúa/Tequila, 112
Cold Dinner Salad, 99
Corn Bread Dressing, 80
Corn/Barley Wine, 65

D

Darrell's Pargo a la Veracruzana, 42
Dried Beef, 41
Dried Meat and Eggs, 9
"Drunken" Chicken, 126

E

Ejote en Chile Colorado, 13
Elote Frito, 43
Empañadas de Calabaza, 82
Encaje Mexicano, 88
Enchiladas, 119
Enchiladas Sonoreñas, 100
Ensalada de Berro, 29
Ensalada de Coditos, 50
Ensalada de Frijoles Negros, 36
Ensalada de Jícama, 49
Ensalada de Nopalitos, 18
Ensalada de Papas, 50

F

Flan, 121
Fresh Salsa, 60
Fried Cabrilla, 37
Frijoles Charros, 93
Frijoles Pintos, 93
Frijoles Refritos, 94

Fudge Frosting, 21
Fruit Smoothies, 47

G

Galletas de Bodas, 51
Ginger Cookies, 118
Great Chile Roast, The, 70
Green Beans with Red Chile, 13
Green Chile Corn Soup, 122
Green Chile Posole, 90
Green Chile Sauce, 57
Green Chile Sauce Chilaquile, 79
Green Chile Stew, 124
Green Corn Tamales, 64
Grilled Steak, 8
Guacamole, 44, 45, 46

H

Hibiscus Tea, 47
Horchata, 34

J

Jamaica, 47
Jericalla a la Madeline, 14
Jericalla de Abuelita, 15
Jicama Salad, 49

L

Licuadas de Frutas, 47
"Lost" Tamal, 133

M

Macaroni with Chorizo, 117
Macaroni Salad, 50
Macarrones con Chorizo, 117
Madeline's Meringue Custard, 14
Marinated Güerito Chiles, 83

Index

Meatball Soup, 72
Meat with Chile, 135
Meringue, 14
Meringue Kisses, 76
Mexican Beef, 85
Mexican Spoon Bread, 91
Mexican Fudge, 125
Mexican Hot Cocoa, 115
Mexican Lace Cookies, 88
Mexican Wedding Cookies, 51

N

Nopalito Salad, 18
Nopalitos con Huevos, 16
Nopalitos con Puerco, 18
Nopalitos with Eggs, 16
Nopalitos with Pork, 18

O

Ochoa Family's Pipián, 97
Old Man's Soup, 130

P

Pan de Elote, 91
Pan de Huevo o Pan Dulce, 19
Papas con Chorizo, 117
Pastel de Chocolate, 21
Pastel de Gallina, 92
Pico de Gallo, 55
Pinto Beans, 93
Pipián de la Familia Ochoa, 97
Pollo Borracho, 126
Pollo en Chile Colorado, 12
Pollo en Mole, 77
Pollo en Pipián con Chile Colorado, 95
Pollo en Pipián con Chile Verde, 96
Pollo Rojo en Hojas de Elote, 22
Posole con Chile Colorado, 90

Posole con Chile Verde, 90
Posole Mexicano, 89, 90
Potato Salad, 50
Potato-Cheese Soup, 98
Potatoes with Chorizo, 117
Pumpkin Turnovers, 82

R

Red Chile Chicken in Corn Husks, 22
Red Chile Marinade, 22
Red Chile Posole, 90
Red Chile Sauce, 56
Red Chile Sauce with Chilaquiles, 78
Red Snapper Veracruz-style, 42
Refried Beans, 94
Relleno de Pan de Elote, 80
Relleno para Pavo o Pollo, 103
Rice Drink, 34
Rice Pudding, 23
Rompope, 127
Rum Eggnog, 127

S

Salpicón, 99
Salsa de Chiltepines, 59
Salsa de Tomatillos, 66
Salsa Fresca, 60
Salsa para Tacos, 63
Sausage, 116, 117
Sautéed Corn, 43
Sautéed Squash, 40
Shredded Beef, 35
Soft Tacos, 62
Sonoran Flat Enchiladas, 100
Sopa de Albóndigas, 72
Sopa de Viejo, 130
Sopaipillas, 102
Sopita de Fideos, 129
Spanish or Mexican Rice, 25
Steamed Rice, 26

Stuffing for Turkey or Chicken, 103
Sweet Bean Tamales, 132
Sweet Bread, 19

T

Taco Sauce, 63
Tacos de Atún, 28
Tacos de Varias Clases, 61
Tacos: Beef, 61; Soft, 62; Chicken, 62
Tamales, 132–37
Tamales de Elote, 64
Tamales Dulces, 132
Tamal Perdido, 133
Teswin, 65

Tomatillo Sauce, 66
Tortilla Soup, 104
Tortillas and Eggs, 27
Tortillas con Huevos, 27
Tostadas, 67
Tuna Tacos, 28

V

Vegetable Beef Soup, 120
Vermicelli Soup, 129

W

Watercress Salad, 29